Conversations
with my dog

Chris Parker

The Science, Art and Magic of Transformational Communication

Chiselbury

Published by Chiselbury Publishing, a division of Woodstock Leasor Limited, 14 Devonia Road, London N1 8JH, United Kingdom

www.chiselbury.com

ISBN: 978-1-916556-11-9

'Reality exists in the space between two people.'
Epiah Khan

'Or in the space between one person and their dog.'
Sam the dog

'If you want to know how to understand and influence others elegantly and repeatedly, Chris Parker is the man to turn to. He is motivational, inspirational and entertaining.'
Caroline Sunderland. PhD. Associate Professor. Reader in Environmental and Sport Physiology. Nottingham Trent University.

'Chris can help anyone improve the communication skills that will enhance both their professional and social life. Chris also teaches effective – and vital – business communication skills. I recommend Chris most highly.'
Gary Anderson. Author. Inspirational Speaker. Counsellor.

'Using the magic of Chris Parker's communication strategies, processes and skills, you will learn quickly how to declutter your mind - and focus on the things that really matter to you. He transforms the way you think and enables you to achieve the most positive of outcomes.'
Lizzie Butler. Business Development and Communication Consultant.

'Chris is masterful at using stories, activities and examples in a seamless, integrated way to change and improve the way people think and act. His understanding of communication and influence is outstanding.'
Dr John Sullivan. Clinical Sport Psychologist/Sport Scientist. Head of Psychology at High Performance Sport New Zealand.

'Communication is the key to unlocking success and happiness in all relationships, and it is a topic in which Chris Parker excels. In this, his latest book, he seamlessly infuses his many years of theoretical and practical knowledge, providing abundant benefits for those wanting to enhance their professional experiences and those seeking stronger relationships at home and between friends.'
Jason Phillips. Director at Wiltons Holdings.

'When it comes to communication, Chris Parker just seems to hit the nail on the head. An amazing communications Guru whose approach just works.'
Andy Fretwell. MCMI. Leisure Manager. Gedling Borough Council.

'Chris Parker is a rare talent. This is an amazing book.'
Eddie Quinn. Professional Martial Arts Instructor. Founder of The Approach.

Acknowledgements

My sincere thanks to:
Stuart for always making the process fun, fast and focused.
Mairi and Alan for their continued, constructive feedback.
Paul Dyson for the original cover art.
Benjamin Hill for the cartoons.
And, of course, to Sam for the conversations, the walks, the lessons - and everything else.

Table of Contents

Pre- Introduction No.1

Welcome to Conversations with my dog.

This is both a teaching book and a story book. The topic is Communication and Influence. It's a topic I began studying in 1976. It's a study that continues to the present day and, like all committed students and practitioners, I've learnt many things from many teachers. Some of them knew that they were playing the role of teacher, some of them didn't. I'm grateful to them all.

What does this book teach?

How to communicate positively and powerfully with yourself and others, using both the spoken and written word, in ways that enable you to achieve your desired outcomes in both the professional and personal aspects of your life.

Why does this teaching book contain stories?

Because teaching through storytelling is an age-old practice. Stories engage our attention, fire our imaginations, promote insight, and help us to recognise connections, in ways that simple facts cannot. The most engaging stories are also memorable.

Why is this teaching book called Conversations with my dog? I can best answer that by:

- Talking about the wonderful significance of conversations.
- Introducing you to my dog, Sam, and explaining the central role he plays in my life and in this book.

Here we go:

The wonderful significance of conversations

Conversations are the building blocks of influence. They are at the heart of our communication. And, as I argue in the next pre-introduction, there's nothing more important in our lives than the quality of our communication.

Conversations happen so frequently, that it's easy to ignore their wonderful significance. Yet such frequency plays a vital role in creating that significance. We don't get through a day without engaging in myriad conversations with ourselves and with others. They will be of varying lengths and importance. Some of the people we have conversations with we will know very well, some might be strangers. These conversations will have different purposes and outcomes. Some might be professional in nature; others might be some purely social. They might be with a single person, or with several. They might be one-off, stand-alone, conversations, or part of an on-going series. Some we might have planned, others will be more free-flowing, an interaction we make up as we go along, in what we can think of as communication-jazz.

Whatever their type or purpose, conversations inevitably influence those involved to some degree.

Sometimes conversations don't work out as expected and can lead to negative consequences if not corrected. Some conversations are so casual, of such an ordinary everyday nature, their influence is barely noticeable and/or quickly forgotten. Others can be life-changing in the most positive of ways.

In all probability, you have experienced such conversations. You might have recognised their significance at the time, or in hindsight. Either way, the odds are that you can quite easily recall magical conversations that transformed your life.

No matter when, where, or how those conversations occurred, they would have been made up of a mix of any, or all, of the following:

- Sounds (For example, words, sighs, laughter.)
- Gestures.
- Silence.
- Breathing.
- Repetition.

- Sequencing.
- Emotion.
- Awareness.
- Attention-giving.

All of which I will address as we go through the book. All of which we can learn to manage ever-more skilfully, so that we create the influence and the outcome(s) we desire, as we progress through our conversation-filled life.

With that said, I'm thrilled to introduce:

Sam the dog

Sam is my ten-year-old Staffordshire Bull Terrier. He is one of two very special Communication teachers I have had in my life. As a teacher, Sam is attentive, alert, congruent, inspiring, and always willing to share a lesson.

You may be surprised to hear that I've learnt many things about Communication and Influence from a Staffordshire Bull Terrier. You might wonder just how it's possible to communicate effectively with someone like Sam who doesn't use the same vocabulary, who experiences the world very differently, has different behaviours and attitudes, and relies heavily on body language to share messages.

You might think that's just about impossible. Or, like me, you might treat having conversations with your dog as an exciting opportunity to improve your communication skills.

After all, how many of the people you know use precisely the same language as you in precisely the same ways? How many of them experience and interpret every event and express emotions just as you do? How many have precisely the same behaviours and attitudes?

In my experience the answer is 'None.'

Just because people living in the same country tend to use the same words and have some agreed gestures and greetings, that doesn't mean they share the same meanings, messages, and feelings in exactly the same way. If that were the case, there wouldn't be any issues caused by miscommunication. And there always are, in every community and in every country.

For example, Sam belongs to a breed that has, in the past, had occasional bad press. It makes some people mistrust Sam, even though they've never spent time with him or any of his brothers and sisters. The truth is, Sam is a loving, loyal, and trustworthy member of our family. He is selfless in his commitment to those he lives with. Yet sometimes his muscular, confident appearance and a few, infrequent headlines, make people misjudge him instantly. That just shows you the power of communication. We need to get it right.[1]

Sam and I do get it right. He teaches me how to have the best possible conversations. We share the full range of sounds, gestures, silence, breathing, repetition, sequencing, emotion, awareness and attention-giving that I listed earlier. We interact, we share an abode and a certain way of life, together we turn, conducting ourselves appropriately in social situations.

And if you're wondering why I've just said all of that, it's because I'm referring to the Latin root of our word 'conversation'. It comes from the verb *conversari*, which is a compound of *con,* meaning 'with' or 'together' and *versare,* meaning 'to turn'. From this verb comes the word, *conversation,* which has several meanings dependent on context. These included, 'conduct', 'a particular, disciplined, habitual form of living', and, of course, 'social interaction and communication'.

---

[1] Personally, I believe there are very few genetically bad dogs; inadequate owners usually cause the problems. I'm sure the same can be said of words. There are very few inherently bad words; there are just unskilled and/or unethical users of words.

So, in all these ways, and for all of these reasons, I can say that Sam and I are great conversationalists. And I've learnt much about communication from the very special conversations that we share. Hence the title of this book. It not only reflects my experience with Sam, it also lets you know that he's going to be communicating with you, too. I'm delighted that, as you turn the pages, and interact with the content, you will find yourself sharing some conversations with my dog. I hope you find them to be as useful, and as much fun, as I do.

You see, despite our differences – or, perhaps, because of them – Sam and I have a very special relationship. I am in charge, but Sam still stays by my side whenever I take the lead. Our time together really is a walk in the park.

'Do you know the best thing about being a dog? It's simple. I know how to trust my natural instincts.'

Pre- Introduction No.2

Why communication is so very, very important, why it always starts before it starts, and some necessary information about me.

Communication is so very, very important because the quality of our interpersonal and intrapersonal communication determines the quality of our entire life experience and influences the life experiences of those with whom we share our time and energy.

I have long-thought that there are essentially two types of communication. I believe these two types hold true no matter what the nature of our communication, whether it is intra-personal (communicating with ourselves) or interpersonal (communicating with others), whether it is an informal conversation, or a formal presentation, whether it is communication shared with individuals, groups, communities or nations.

The two types are:

- Transactional.
- Transformative.

Whilst these are not mutually exclusive – communication can be transactional and transformative simultaneously – I will, by way of introduction and explanation, address them individually.

Transactional communication

This is the language of deals, trade-offs, and agreements. When people in the business world ask me to provide communication training, it's primarily so that I can improve their transactional communication. I understand the need for that. It's what shapes economies, puts money in our pockets, grows our careers.

Transactional communication isn't limited only to that context, though. It also plays a part in our social lives. We often persuade others, negotiate with loved ones, agree a little give-and-take. Transactional communication can be caring and loving, motivated by the most positive of emotions and purposes. What defines it, however, is the inevitability of some form of deal.

The best of deals can be summarised as win-win activities, in which all parties involved gain some benefit. Whilst the worst type of transactional communication creates winners and losers. It is a competition, the results of which benefit only one party.

Sam doesn't do that type of transactional communication. He never stops caring about those with whom he is communicating; he never has an agenda he pushes forward at the expense of others. Of course, he lets me know when he's hungry or wants a walk. He has needs, as we all do, and he trusts that I will respect them. He, in turn, respects my needs and those of my family. Our transactions with Sam are all win-win.

Although I value and use transactional communication, it is not the main reason for my lifelong study. Conversations, and all other forms of communication, don't have power just because they create transactions. In fact, their greatest power isn't transactional.

Ultimately, communication is so very, very important because it can be transformational.

Transformational communication

Communication in all its forms can be transformative because it affects our brains. We are influenced by the words and gestures of others, by their breathing and facial expressions. Our words, gestures, breathing and facial expressions influence others. That's why we must be respectful and accepting of the responsibility we have whenever we communicate.[2]

Used brilliantly, communication can create positive changes in peoples' sense of self-identity, their abilities and levels of performance, their relationships and their communities.

The transformative power of communication presents us with our greatest opportunity and our greatest challenge. We can use conversations to shape, change, create and improve our own life experience and that of others. Or, if we get it wrong, we can do the opposite. Just as transactional communication can create losers, so inappropriate intrapersonal and interpersonal communication can transform lives in the most negative of ways.

Sam, of course, is a super-positive transformer! He has been from his first day with us. He is always alert to the first signs of our joy, accomplishment, fatigue, negativity or upset. He responds accordingly in a heartbeat. Through his example, he teaches the humans in the house that our purpose is to help each other share, express, and grow in the best of ways; to be encouraging, supportive, adaptable, and strong.

Even though we can't be perfect.

And we can't.

We can't communicate perfectly, just as we can't do anything else perfectly, so we need to be ready and willing to recognise and learn from our mistakes. Feedback offers the antidote to error. It contains the seeds for correction and transformation. Feedback literally feeds and fuels our conversations.

It does this because conversations, just like all forms of communication, are an interactive feedback loop. They are an endless spiral of energy and transmission that can, at their best, transform even the worst of situations.

When we know how to harness and use the power of

---

[2] More about how communication influences our brain in the next chapter.

conversations, our communication becomes shared and meaningful.

Our relationships, our skills, our ability to teach, learn and grow, the career path we take, our dreams and goals, our values, beliefs, and worldview, are all influenced by the conversations we share, and those we have shared.

Our conversations ripple out, like waves on the surface of the water, sometimes extending beyond the horizon of our own awareness. The currents they create, whether intended or not, can be subtle, gentle, obvious, challenging or, even, threatening. Our conversations have the power to clash and roar, or to soothe and relax; to lead gently, or to grab and drive forcefully.

If we downplay the power of our conversations, if we forget or deny this ripple-effect, we not only reject an essential part of our humanity and our connection with others, we also turn our backs on the responsibility we have in influencing our world.

In the coming pages, I'll consider how communication connects and affects us. I'll also share examples that highlight the power of conversations and show why we need to use that power with elegance, skill, and a genuine care for all involved. For now, though, let's just say that communication is so very, very important because:

Communication shapes the present and creates the future.

And we owe it to ourselves, to those we love and those we serve, to know how to make the present brilliant and the future bright.

With that said, let's dip briefly into the past.

Epiah Khan, pre-introductions and me

In the late 1800's, Epiah Khan, the apocryphal Middle Eastern mystic, wrote *It starts before it starts* and I'm pretty sure he knew that he was going to write it before he did.

He went on to explain that every process has steps that occur before the so-called start. In the world of communication, we can think of these steps as pre-introductions.

Pre-introductions are the bits that precede the obvious beginning. They are the bits through which we start before we make it clear that we've started. Their purpose is to set the tone and the context, and to begin changing the state of those with whom we are communicating. Pre-introductions are mechanisms of influence. They are used widely and often.

For example, we experience them when we go to the theatre, most obviously when a voice lets us know that 'Tonight's show will begin in twenty minutes,' before doing a gradual countdown designed to heighten our excitement and ensure we get to our seat in time. The pre-introductions then continue with a reminder to switch off our mobile phone, a dimming of the lights, the playing of music and, if appropriate, an enthusiastic voice saying, 'Please welcome to the stage...'

We also experience pre-introductions every time we go into a brilliant restaurant, or to an organisation that understands how to manage its perimeters and greet and treat visitors, or when we are studying in great centres of education, or sitting in the audience of a well-planned business presentation. There are countless other examples. Once you start looking and listening for pre-introductions, you'll appreciate just how frequently they are used to influence us.[3]

Usually, though, when people are using pre-introductions, they don't want them to be recognised. Rather, they want their pre-introductions to ease us away from our normal, everyday world and into theirs without us realising what's happening. And, if they have our wellbeing at heart, I welcome their use

---

[3] For example, the next time you take a flight, notice the many and varied pre-introductions you experience before you board the plane and then again when you have.

of pre-introductions. I want to be eased and moved, changed even, by people who are adding value to my life.

Pre-introductions in a book also help you to ease away from the rest of your day and focus on what's to follow. They give you a feeling for what's to come. They let you settle down and settle in before the obvious beginning of the story.

So, if you haven't already done so, please settle in now whilst I share eight relevant things about me.

They are:

1. I believe that sometimes it is appropriate to treat very important subjects, including the power of conversations, in a light-hearted way.
2. I believe that the quality of both our professional and personal lives depend upon our ability to communicate with each other and with ourselves.
3. I know that, in the workplace, and the home, we can have all the right resources – human, technical, financial and all the rest – and communicate so inappropriately we fail to maximise their potential.
4. I love the fact that every time I improve my communication skills, I improve the quality of my personal and professional life.
5. I love the fact that every time I improve my communication skills, I get to know myself a little better.
6. Although I teach and train others, first and foremost I am a student of interpersonal and intrapersonal communication. It is a study that will continue until I can no longer give skilled attention.
7. I love conversations.
8. I love walking in the park with Sam.

Pre-Introduction No.3

Walking, words and our amazing social brain!

Of course, the phrase 'a walk in the park' can be understood both literally and figuratively.

I mean both.

Because Sam is so skilled, he makes our relationship, and my learning, joyous and easy. And we do spend a great deal of our time walking in the local park. It's where Sam reminds me that becoming an increasingly skilled communicator is simply a step-by-step process.

I hope this book will be a walk in the park for you, too. I hope you will keep returning to it with the same joyous curiosity and clarity that Sam demonstrates whenever he returns to the park. I hope it helps you to achieve your personal and professional goals and enhances your ability to shape your present and brighten your future.

Words are at the heart of doing both because they are central to our conversations.

Words are man-made sounds and symbols that we have agreed to share. Yet these sounds and symbols play a most significant role in sculpting the people we become and the world we build. Just think about it for a moment.

Words create our agreements and our disagreements, our networks and sometimes our isolation. Words build bonds that last a lifetime and can start wars that destroy generations. Words can build families, communities, businesses, and careers, but can also end them in a heartbeat. Words can heal or hurt, encourage or discourage, teach or torture. Words shape our world.

Why do words and how we deliver them have such power?

Because of the ways they affect the human brain.

You see, our brains are wired for us to socialise. Our survival and success as a species are based to a very great degree on our ability to create and maintain positive, collaborative relationships. And words are central to that process.

Here are a few relevant and important brain facts:

- We have big brains relative to our body size, with the average human brain weighing around three pounds.
- It has two sides, seven lobes and billions of inter-connected neurons creating countless neural associations.
- These associations vary according to the stimuli we experience.
- On-going stimulation changes our brain – physically, functionally, and chemically – throughout our lifetime.

Words are one of the most frequent and powerful stimuli. Which is why:

The words you hear and use actually change your brain.

And you don't have to take my words for it. Dr Louis Cozolino, Professor of Psychology at Pepperdine University California, describes the human brain as a social organ of adaptation that grows through our interactions with others.[4]

So, how do words physically change our brain?

According to Dr Cozolino:

'Contact with others...stimulates neural activation, which influences the internal environment of our neurons. This activation in turn triggers the growth of new neurons as well as the transcription of protein, which builds neurons as they expand, connect and organize into functional networks.'

Our brain, then, responds to powerful and/or repeated stimuli

---

[4] Cozolino, L. Neuroscience Psychotherapy. Healing The Social Brain. 2010. W.W.Norton & Company.

by creating new neural associations or pathways. Consequently, we then experience new feelings and create new understandings and behaviours.

A simple way to think of this is:

Stimulus + association = meaning.

Back in the 1970s, when I first started learning about communication and influence, it seemed logical to assume that, when sharing words, we were seeking to influence another person's brain. Only back then, for me, it was an assumption. Now, thanks to the brilliant research of others, we know it to be true.

And if you ever wondered why our brain is so large relative to our body size, the answer is:

We have large brains in order to socialise.

Indeed, the greatest indicator of brain size, particularly the outermost layer known as the neocortex, is the size of the social group in which the species lives.

And, as human beings, we do live within some large and varied social groups.

It's essential that we do. Our ability to interact and work well with others has proven critical in our evolutionary success. We are the dominant species on the planet not because we are the biggest, the strongest or the fastest, but because we're able to solve problems through our social collaborations.

In fact, our social life is so important we tend to think about it whenever we are alone and have a free moment or two.

The question this raises is, do we instinctively think of social matters during our spare time because we experience so many social interactions, or because our brain has evolved to do this? The answer is the latter. We think like this because of a system within our brain known as the default mode network.

This network is another powerful indication of the fact that we are inherently social beings and that strong social bonds provide many short and long-term benefits, both personal and professional.

The flip side of this is that we feel pain whenever we experience social rejection. And it is real pain. It hurts in just the same way that straining a muscle or breaking a bone hurt. That's because social pain and physical pain are both experienced when a part of your brain called the dorsal anterior cingulate cortex is activated. It's found towards the top and the front of the brain. Researchers have discovered that the more pain we feel, whether social or physical, the more the dACC is activated.

If you've ever felt bad because you weren't offered the job you applied for, or the beautiful person in the bar didn't want to know you, or because you weren't picked for the team, or invited to the party, you were feeling a natural pain.

It's a pain that, unlike the hurt of physical injury, often raises all sorts of unpleasant questions and doubts about our self-worth and sense of identity. Breaking your leg rarely, if ever, threatens your sense of belonging. Indeed, it can often bring welcome support. Whereas the pain of rejection can both hurt and isolate. It's so powerful we don't even need to be rejected by people we know or like to experience it.

If you are wondering why our brain actively ensures that we feel pain in such circumstances, it's because our survival and success depend on our ability to socialise and work collaboratively. The more we stay together, the better we are likely to do. It makes sense, then, for rejection to hurt. That motivates us to avoid it. That means we instinctively value, and therefore work hard to maintain, our relationships with others. This reflects another brain function that's vitally important in regard to communication:

Our brain ensures we feel emotions before we think rationally.

And when I say we, I mean you, me, all of us.

Research suggests we experience hundreds of different

emotional responses every day.

So, whether you like it or not, we are emotional beings who feel emotion before we engage in logical thinking.

Why?

Because our brain's primary task is to ensure our survival, and emotions play a vital role in this. Emotions are signals from the brain, intended to help direct our behaviour. They serve as swift and powerful indicators, helping us to decide what is safe and what isn't, what we should do and what we shouldn't, whom we can trust and whom we can't. We've probably all had the experience of our gut instinct telling us how to treat a stranger; that feeling that either says, 'Yes, I can trust you,' or 'No, I'll never trust you no matter what.'

Emotions provide the green light to go or flash the red warning light urging us to stop or turn in the other direction.

The parts of our brain responsible for our emotional responses are known collectively as the limbic system. This incorporates the hypothalamus, hippocampus and amygdala along with several other nearby areas of the brain.

The hypothalamus regulates how we respond to our emotions. One way to think of it is as the body's thermostat, regulating responses ranging from hunger, thirst, sexual satisfaction and aggression to blood pressure, digestion and breathing. When, for example, your heartbeat increases and your breathing quickens as you feel a sudden rush of fear, your hypothalamus is at work.

The hippocampus appears to be essential in the creation of long-term memories. This is a vital task. Those of us with a fully functioning hippocampus probably take our memories for granted. Individuals who suffer from a damaged hippocampus cannot access memories. And, as they cannot remember anything, they cannot cope with everyday life.

The amygdala is made up of two almond-shaped masses of neurons. It functions as the relay station for emotional processing. Because of the amygdala's connections within the brain, it not only operates as the centre for identifying danger and creating a flight or fight response, it also influences our expressions of other emotions such as affection and love.

Yet our brain does not work alone in creating our emotions. It interacts with both the stomach and the heart via the vagus nerve. This is a nerve that is rooted in the cerebellum and the brainstem, and wanders down into our abdomen, connecting with our heart and most other major organs along the way. That's why we experience those so-called gut instincts that I mentioned a moment ago.

And, because words affect brains, they create powerful, often compelling, emotional responses. That's why words have power. That's why the quality of our conversations is so important. That's why I hope you'll join me and my four-legged guru for a walk in our park.

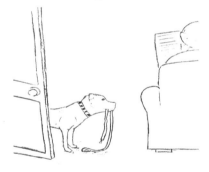

'Reading a book can be as exciting as going for a walk in the park. Only you shouldn't need to relieve yourself straight away.'

The Introduction

The nature and purpose of communication, the principles of influence, the nature of words and when words have the most power.

The nature and purpose of communication

I'm going to offer you two definitions of communication. One now and the other at the end of Chapter One. The first definition explains both the nature and the purpose of communication. It reads:

> *Communication is an interactive feedback loop that operates as our primary method of exchange.*

The four elements of this loop are: the sender; the message; the receiver; the feedback.

As communication never occurs in a vacuum, there are inevitably distractions and unforeseen influences in the environment. These can be thought of as 'noise'. Examples include:

- People with different ideologies or agendas sharing opposing messages to our own.
- Social changes.
- Personal and professional pressures.
- The influence of such factors as memories, beliefs, hopes or fears.

It's because of this noise that our words can, for example, unintentionally stir a memory in someone's mind, or remind them of an upcoming event, or create an unwanted emotional response.

Although skilled communicators know how to silence or, at least, limit their own, personal noise, the inevitability of distractions and unforeseen influences is the reason why we cannot ever fully control any form of communication.

The most skilled communicators, and Sam is a great example of this, are alert for the influence of noise – both positive and negative. They are curious enough to explore, to seek feedback and clarification, enabling them to adapt their communication if necessary.

This is one of the reasons why:

Every communication provides learning.

And the learning we get from every communication changes us if we let it. We come to realise that our beliefs, expectations, goals, desires and all the other factors about ourselves that we tend to take for granted[5] are simply mechanisms we use for getting through today. As we manage the inevitability of noise, and communicate and influence others, we are, in turn, influenced.

So, before we go any further in our walk through this particular park, do remember always that:

Communication is a complex rather than a linear interaction.

Through the communication interactive feedback loop, we exchange ideas and information, beliefs, thoughts and feelings. We seek to explain ourselves to others and, in turn, gain insights into them. Amongst other things, we learn, teach, soothe, heal, encourage, motivate, sell, persuade, punish, reward and lead. We defend and promote those causes we support and oppose those we don't.

Our ability to manage that interactive feedback loop determines our value as a partner, parent, friend, boss, expert, advisor, elder, colleague, counsellor, teammate and all the other roles we assume throughout our lives.

Interestingly, most of us think we're pretty good at

---

[5] More about these later.

communicating. Actually, many of us think we're very good at it. A colleague and I once surveyed over 600 men and women of different ages from a wide range of professions. We asked them the simple question: 'How good are you at communicating?'

More than 70% rated themselves as 'Good' or 'Very Good' and over 8% rated themselves as 'Excellent' communicators.

We then asked our respondents to score the importance of communication in both their personal and professional lives.

Once again, the vast majority were in no doubt, with 80% reporting that their ability to communicate well was either 'Very important' or 'Essential' in the workplace, and 78% describing it as 'Very important' or 'Essential' in their personal lives.

This came as no surprise. Numerous surveys have revealed that communication skills are regarded as being of vital importance in all aspects of our lives. Not only that, educational establishments offer courses in all aspects of communication, and businesses across sectors stress the importance of great communication. We all seem to know how important it is.

And yet the evidence suggests that we're not as good at managing conversations and the power of words as we believe we are. And the effects of miscommunication are costly and sometimes devastating.

Here are the results of just a few relevant surveys and reports:

- A survey of companies with around 100 staff found that inadequate communication cost each company an average of $420,000 per annum.[6]

---

[6] David Grossman. The Cost of Poor Communication. The Holmes Report.

- The cost of inadequate communication in companies with 100,000 employees rose to an average of $62.4 million![7]
- Miscommunication in the UK's National Health Service, including poor communication between GPs and hospitals, leads to medication errors that contribute to as many as 23,000 deaths a year.[8]
- Communication problems have been cited as the main reason for divorce.[9]

Communication problems also cause once loyal customers to walk away from a brand, children to turn their backs on education, family members to feel misunderstood, friendships to break down, individuals to doubt their capabilities, teams to underperform and, even, communities to fracture.

Sometimes all it takes is just one communication error to create a negative and wholly unintended outcome. Let's take a business example, that of a customer who shops in the same supermarket once a week and has done so for the last five years. Each week our imaginary shopper spends £100 in the store. Until one day a miscommunication occurs between them and a staff member. Inappropriate words are said, and our shopper decides to end their connection with the supermarket.

Not such a big deal, you might say.

Until we put some numbers to the cost of this miscommunication. Our shopper has been spending £400 a

[7] As for 6.

[8] Prevalence and Economic Burden of Medication Errors in the NHS in England. Elliott R, Camacho E, Campbell F, Jankovic D, Martyn St James M, Kaltenhaler E, Wong R, Sculpher M, Faria R. (2018)

[9] Reported reasons for breakdown of marriage and Cohabitation in Britain: Findings from the third National Survey of Sexual Attitudes and Lifestyles.

month for the last five years. Let's say they only do this for 10 months of the year, as they are away the rest of the time. That's a total spend of £4000 per annum. As they expect to stay in their house until their children move out (which, given their ages, will be a minimum of 10 years), the supermarket has just lost £40,000 at current prices.

Only it's worse than that. Research suggests that unhappy customers are far more likely to talk about their negative experiences than satisfied customers are about theirs.[10] Our shopper tells 10 others. It's enough to persuade one to also shop elsewhere. Given that this person's average spend was £300 per month and that they, too, would have used the supermarket for many years to come, that's another loss that adds up to tens of thousands of pounds. And then, of course, this shopper tells the story to 9 others, one of whom shares it with their 380 Facebook friends...

Now, I'm not suggesting for a moment that the price paid for this particular mismanagement of words is anything like as significant as those paid when people die because of medical communication errors, or when relationships are ended, or when families are forced to separate. However, successful businesses are the beating economic heart of every community in every country. Our imaginary supermarket couldn't afford to take such repeated losses. And the community it serves needs it, and all the other local businesses, to succeed.

This is just one of many scenarios and, when considered all together, the varied costs of miscommunication lead us to an inevitable conclusion:

---

[10] Different research carried out in different markets at different times suggests that unhappy customers tell between 9 and 20 other people, whereas happy customers tell as few as 3 others.

We are not always as good at communicating as we think we are.

Why do we overestimate our ability?
Perhaps because:

- We do get some good results – and, indeed, some great ones – and we tend to focus on these, exaggerating their frequency.
- The negative results of our miscommunication often happen later and, because we don't experience them quickly and directly, it's easy to avoid connecting them to our inappropriate words.
- We blame the other person/people for any breakdown in communication.
- Most of us have never experienced any rigorous, in-depth communication training, so we simply don't know what we don't know.
- Consequently, we feel that we are good enough.

What causes miscommunication?
There is no simple answer to this. The most common causes include:

- The lack of an appropriate desired outcome.
- Not understanding those with whom we are communicating.
- Not realising that people do things for their reasons, not ours.
- The use of the wrong language and content.
- The use of the wrong communication channel(s).
- Distractions within the environment. (The noise I mentioned earlier).

These causes can operate individually but are often interconnected. We can avoid them all through audience analysis.

Audience analysis

We need to use skilled attention-giving[11] to identify the starting point of those with whom we are communicating.

This starting point encompasses:

- Their knowledge, understanding, beliefs, hopes and fears regarding the topic we are addressing.
- Their self-image and how they wish to be regarded and treated.
- Their preferred language patterns and communication channels.
- The particular influencers they give credence to.

These are all examples of perception filters.

Perception filters determine how we experience the world. They are created through our socialisation, education and experience. They include beliefs, about everything from politics and religion to the meaning of life and why you love your favourite sports team, values, memories, language, perceptions of time and personal habits.

Perception filters operate like invisible spectacles, creating a taken-for-granted worldview. The effect of these spectacles is to increase the likelihood that we will see and interpret the same event, speech or situation differently from at least some of those around us.

Every message we send passes through the perception filters of those with whom we are communicating. Unless we are highly skilled at managing our own state, every reply they make is filtered by us in a similar way. These filters influence the way we decode every message.

Being a successful communicator means creating messages

---

[11] Lots more about skilled attention-giving coming shortly.

that are most likely to be received as intended, whilst monitoring our own responses to ensure that we don't suffer from 'filter distortion'.

This distortion occurs because, in every form of communication, there is a gap in transmission, during which time the information is filtered according to a person's worldview. We can think of this gap as the 'communication synapse'.

Our choice, then, is simple. We can either analyse our audience, identifying their perception filters, and increasing our chances of sharing messages that cross the communication synapse in ways that inspire the desired reaction. Or do no analysis and run the risk that our communication is distorted through the other person's perceptual filters.

Now, you might be thinking that insightful audience analysis is fine if there is plenty of time before the communication will take place, but that it can't be done during the immediacy of a conversation – especially with a stranger.

Whilst it is easier if we can prepare in advance, I assure you a genuine level of insight can be achieved in only a matter of moments if you know how to listen, look and question. We will address how to do this in the coming chapters.

For now, suffice to say that analysis enables you to:

- Determine your audience's current state, their understanding of the situation and their language preferences.
- Begin your communication with content that makes sense to them.

By doing this, we share the message:

'I respect you and I'm learning to understand you.'

And when we do get our communication right the results can be amazing! In the workplace successful communication impacts positively in myriad ways. For example, it:

- Is at the core of great leadership.
- Creates and builds client relationships.
- Promotes the brand.
- Underpins business growth.
- Increases employee engagement.
- Encourage and/or helps to maintain wellbeing.
- Develops a sense of belonging.
- Mitigates conflict.
- Develops networks.
- Builds high-performing teams.
- Motivates staff.
- Creates individual feelings of self-worth and value.

Whilst, in our personal lives, it helps us to:

- Create and develop a powerful bond with our life partner.
- Guide, develop and support our children.
- Share emotions appropriately.
- Be a role model.
- Build enduring friendships.
- Create emotionally secure environments.
- Manage uncertainty and change.
- Support others during challenging times.
- Manage loss.
- Influence family relationships positively.
- Create supportive, respectful communities.
- Balance successfully the many different aspects of our life experience.

The bottom line is, the nature, value and success of both our professional and personal relationships, are determined by the quality and appropriateness of our communication.

Conversations are central to this; they are integral to our entire life experience. They fill the moment. They live in the memories of others. They can change tomorrow. They are the source of our influence.

The principles of influence

Before we consider the principles, let's just quickly ask and answer the question, what is influence?

The word stems from the Latin word *influentum,* meaning a 'flowing in'. This was the root of the Old French word *influence,* used to describe an ethereal power believed to flow in from the stars. Nowadays we think of influence as the power we possess to affect change on ourselves, our environment and others.

We create influence by our presence, the conversations we have and the words we share. Our communication flows into, and therefore impacts upon, the life experience of those around us.

It does this because there is no uninfluential communication. Whenever someone's brain is aware of us, we influence. Sometimes they are aware of it consciously. Sometimes they are not. Either way, we affect their emotional and physical state to some degree.

The inevitability of influence is clear every time someone meets Sam for the first time. It doesn't matter if they are in the same room as him, or if they pass him on the street, or see him playing in the park, there is always a reaction. Some people immediately want to greet him. Others are more cautious. Some just admire how handsome he is.

Whilst we might not all create such obvious responses, we are all powerful influencers.

And, according to the research of Professor Robert Cialdini, the Regents' Professor Emeritus of Psychology and Marketing at Arizona State University, there are seven key principles of influence. These are:

- Likeness.

- Reciprocity.
- Commitment and consistency.
- Authority.
- Scarcity.
- Social proof.
- Unity.

Let's consider them one at a time:

Likeness

Research shows that the more we like someone, the more easily we are influenced by them. Matching another person's communication patterns is a particularly powerful way to create likeness. We can use it to create rapport incredibly swiftly, to make the instinctive gut response that I mentioned earlier a positive one.[12]

Reciprocity

This refers to the practice of exchanging things for mutual benefit and/or due to feelings of indebtedness. Research indicates that if you do someone a favour they will, in all probability, return it. They might even return it with interest! So, if you want someone to do something for you, do something for them first.

Commitment and Consistency

Simply put, people are more likely to act in a consistent manner once they have made a commitment to do so. Interestingly, this is the case even if the original incentive for doing so has been removed.

The lesson is: make it easy for people to commit to you, your

---

[12] I'll explain how to do that in Chapter Three.

cause, your idea, your plan, or your product, and acknowledge their commitment repeatedly, before encouraging them towards an even greater commitment.

Authority

If we accept a person as a figure of authority, we tend to do what they ask of us. An individual can claim such power because of their personal charisma, their acknowledged expertise in a given arena, their social status, or their professional role.

It follows therefore that the more you are regarded as an authoritative figure, the more influence you automatically wield.

Scarcity

One way to create the public perception of value is to limit the availability of a particular product or service. If a restaurant is fully booked for the next two months, it's easy to presume that it must be excellent. If we are told that the antique we own is the last of its kind, we assume immediately that it will be worth a great deal of money.

When a business has a unique selling point that cannot be matched, it has a scarcity that adds significant value. When an individual demonstrates a unique competency, they do the same.

Social proof

This is a phrase first used by Cialdini in 1984. It describes the way people are drawn to copy the actions and attitudes of the majority. Social proof is an extremely powerful influencer. It can install beliefs, shape attitudes, and improve, limit, or prevent certain behaviours.

At its best, the power of social proof draws people together to support a Civil Rights movement even in the face of aggression and violence. At its worst, it can lead to genocide.

Both Martin Luther King and Adolf Hitler knew how to use the power of communication to create social proof.

They both remind us that communication affects brains, creates emotions and incites action. They remind us, for very different reasons, about the powerful, life-changing nature of words.

So does Cialdini's final principle:

Unity

This is the powerful feeling of connection, of community, of 'us-ness', that our communication and conversations can create, and which, in turn, influence our decision-making and our actions.

As with the preceding principles, Unity can be created for a variety of reasons, to achieve a variety of outcomes.[13]

The nature of words

There are no passive words.

Words do far more than simply identify or describe.

Words can change laws and create wars. They provide or reinforce the lens through which we view the world and make sense of it. Words are the solidifiers and change-makers of human existence.

That's why I believe we have an ethical responsibility to use words with absolute care and attention, respecting the right of others to be free from selfish, manipulative, and potentially harmful influence.

We are living in an age when the power of words to create new futures is explicit.

---

[13] If you want to know more about Cialdini's work, I suggest you read: Cialdini, R. Influence, New and Expanded: The Psychology of Persuasion. 2021. Harper Bus.

Whether or not words are being used to create the best of all possible futures is open to debate.

I've already mentioned some of the costs of miscommunication. There is, though, a world of difference between an unintended communication error and the deliberate use of words – a communication plan – designed to mislead, misdirect and benefit the few at the expense of the many.

Rollo May, an American psychologist, wrote that effective communication:

'...leads to community; that is, to understanding, intimacy and mutual valuing.'[14]

Tragically, though, it seems that for some people effective communication means simply getting their own way, no matter what the cost to others.

I've always thought that words have the same power and potential as a brilliantly engineered car. Like the car, words move us; they influence the journeys we take and the routes we make throughout our life. Like the car, words can provide comfort and support along the way. Like the car, words can be appreciated and admired. And, like the car, if words are mishandled, they can blind us to much of life's journey; leaving us inappropriately focused on ourselves and our own speed of travel. Worst of all, if mishandled, either by accident or design, words, just like the car, can be destructive.

Although we may not all be drivers, we are all communicators. We all have the responsibility of learning how to use the power of words to steer a course that enhances our life whilst, at the

---

[14] May, R. Power and Innocence: A Search for the Sources of Violence. 1998. W. W. Norton & Company.

very least, keeping everyone else safe. Thus, we need to know:

When words have the most power

Words have the most power when:

- We have a clearly defined desired outcome.
- We understand those we seek to influence.
- We are acknowledged as an appropriate messenger.
- We are in the best possible communication state.
- We understand that influence is emotional first, and we create positive emotional responses in others.
- We sequence the right words appropriately.
- We use the most appropriate communication channels.
- We turn our words into engaging stories that share meaningful messages and include supporting facts.
- We know how and when to repeat our story.
- We create more-the-more patterns of agreement.
- We seek out feedback and respond to it appropriately.

To use these eleven elements effectively, we first need to develop and apply the most relevant attitudes and attributes. That's what the next chapter is all about.

'It's a new day! What can be more wonderful than that?'

Chapter One

Being a Skilled Communicator (i)

The attitudes and attributes that enable us to harness and use the power of conversations.

In this chapter I'm going to talk about scallops, silence, space, meditation, walls, triangles, curtains, forgetfulness, and some other things I can't remember right now. However, before I do, I need to address the strapline for this book.

To save you looking back at the cover, it reads: 'The Science, Art and Magic of Transformational Communication.'

Science is essentially the study of the natural and social world and all associated behaviours. Scientists share with us the knowledge of their research.

I've talked already about the ongoing research into the power of words on human interaction. Through this, science is helping us to understand more and more about how and why we are such powerful influencers. We, in turn, can use this understanding to communicate ever more powerfully, ethically and elegantly.

Definitions of art refer to the making of images, objects, music or performances that express ideas and/or emotions. Art, then, is a form of communication.

I'm particularly drawn to the painter Edgar Degas' definition of art. He said: 'Art is not what you see, but what you make others see.'

I'm drawn to it because conversations can be used to change what others see, and it can be done with such subtlety that, whilst a new perspective is created and acknowledged, the actual influencing process remains hidden. This, I suggest, is a form of high art.

When we combine science and art, we create magic. By which I mean the use of special, sometimes hidden, powers that create movement and change in ways the majority can neither see nor understand. The magical possibilities contained within the power of conversations and other forms of communication are both super and natural. They are ours for the taking – and the giving – if we learn how to become Communication Magicians.

We all have the potential. It's in our DNA.

The DNA of successful communication

This is quite simply:

- **D**esire
- **N**eed
- **A**ttention-giving.

Desire

This is the starting point. If you don't have the desire to become a better communicator, you never will.

The one thing all great communicators have in common is a strong, aligned motivation. They have a fierce, focused desire. This is often the result of a powerful cause. Alan Barnard, a world-leading campaigner of communications, defines cause as:

'...the pursuit of an outcome, a principle or an aim that will improve at least some aspect of a current situation. Moreover, it is the emotional compulsion behind that pursuit. It provides the motivation and the courage for you to campaign for the improvement, and it allows you to share it with others thus enabling them to agree with your improvement and thus to take the action(s) required for you to succeed.'

Once again, the role of emotion is front and centre. Not only does our communication influence others emotionally, our own emotional state determines the nature and direction of the communication we share. Appropriate emotions, it seems, drive us towards satisfying our needs.

Need

In the hierarchy of importance, needs are more significant than wants and wants are more significant than likes. Need satisfaction implies an urgency that just wanting to have something doesn't. It's essential that our needs are met; it's nice when what we'd like to happen actually does.

Whenever we have a powerful emotional compulsion to achieve a specific outcome, we usually turn to the power of communication, conversations and influence to help us achieve it.

The first step in that process takes us back to the importance of audience analysis. For our analysis to be insightful, we must take our awareness and turn it into attention-giving – and that requires certain attitudes and skills.

Skilled attention-giving (i)

Dictionaries define awareness as the conscious ability to perceive or know something. At the most basic level, this means knowing someone, or something, is present.

There are, of course, deeper levels of perception and knowing. To achieve these, we need to give skilled attention. We need to know what to listen and look for, and how to interpret these things accurately.

The relationship between, and transition from, awareness to skilled attention-giving, can be summarised as follows:

Awareness = I know you are present (and that is sufficient).

Skilled attention-giving = I'm motivated to understand you (and I know how to do this).

The ability to give skilled attention begins with the desire to do so, which, in turn, stems from respectful curiosity about those with whom we are communicating.

In my experience, the state that enables skilled attention-giving is a thoughtless process, free – or as free as is humanly possible – from the influence of our own perception filters, any conscious expectations, and any other distractions. (The noise I mentioned earlier.)

To achieve this state, we need to be so interested in the other person, or people, that we temporarily forget about whatever is happening in our life.

The goal is to focus entirely on the other, whether this is an individual, a group, a large audience or a community.

Sam is a master of this. He always gives his complete focus to whomever, or whatever, has drawn his attention. It's natural for him, and, because he's never distracted, because he always forgets himself totally when engaging with others, it took me years to realise the lesson he was sharing.[15]

When I finally did, it completely changed my experience of conversations, and my ability to influence them. I found myself becoming aware of the communication flow as it was happening. I came to understand more clearly my part within that flow, and how to influence its pace, power, expression and/or direction; how to create a powerful sense of connection and relationship.

The best communicators use skilled attention-giving to bridge the communication gap that exists whenever people differentiate between themselves and others. This type of differentiation creates a Me and You approach that can reinforce division. By giving skilled attention, the most

---

[15] Through my years of practice, I've come to understand that the phrase 'It was hidden in plain sight' is misleading. My experience is that nothing is ever hidden in plain sight; rather, we just lack the sensory acuity – the skilled attention-giving – to see or hear it. Sam's lesson on focusing completely on the other is a good example of this. He demonstrated it repeatedly. It was in plain sight. I was just slow in giving it skilled attention.

successful communicators gain insights they can then use to create a sense of Us. Differences, whilst perhaps acknowledged, no longer divide. Consequently, the sense of community and feelings of mutual understanding, that Rollo May highlighted are developed.

I'll talk more about forgetting ourselves, focusing on the other, and transforming Me and You into Us, in the coming pages. I'll also offer a range of practical activities that can help create the state from which we can give skilled attention.

For now, though, I'd like to share one other important point:

Skilled attention-giving is a gift.

We give skilled-attention, and it is best given freely, willingly and joyously. In doing so we not only demonstrate our respect and care for others, we also increase the likelihood of successful interactions because:

Skilled attention-giving is the lifeblood of all great communication.

Skilled attention-giving (ii)

We are sensory beings. We see, hear, feel, smell and taste our experiences. We do this both consciously and subconsciously. Some of us prioritise specific senses or favour certain sense combinations. This occurs instinctively, or because of our training, or because of the context we are in.

It follows, therefore, that the more acute our senses, the greater our ability to give skilled attention. And, just because we have eyes, it doesn't automatically follow that we know how to look with acuity and insight. Just as having ears doesn't automatically make us great listeners. This is equally true, of course, for all our senses; having them and using them habitually doesn't guarantee any great standard of refinement. Let me give you just one example of this:

I have a friend who is a 2 Michelin star chef. He is a culinary genius. He has an understanding of food, and a relationship with it, that I cannot even imagine.

One day I asked him to do some imagining. I asked him to imagine that he was eating a strawberry. He obliged. I watched him feel the non-existent fruit in his mouth then bite into it and experience the burst of flavour. I watched as his lips, tongue and the inside of his mouth changed in response to the sensation he was creating. I watched as his facial skin and his eyes changed, too. I realised at that moment that, despite the fact I had been eating food all my life, I had never tasted food in the way he does.

We talked about this further and it quickly became clear that he recognised far more flavours and textures than I ever had. His experience of eating one single strawberry, whether real or imagined, was far more comprehensive and insightful than my own. Indeed later, in his kitchen, he pointed to his latest intake of scallops, received from his Scottish supplier, and said, 'Chris, if you really want to learn how to cook, begin by learning how to listen to food. You have to open that scallop and hear what it's telling you. I mean hear it! Properly! You really must listen!'

I'd been a fool to presume that because I had a nose, mouth and tongue I could smell and taste food as he did. He was an extremely skilled professional who had worked to develop his sensory acuity. I just liked to eat and drink. Ultimately, that's why I pay him to do the cooking.

This difference is equally true in the world of interpersonal communication.

Only the world of interpersonal communication is our social world. We don't need a strawberry or a scallop to help us develop our sensory acuity and awareness. We can do it every time we walk down the street, or go into a shop, or sit in a bar, or travel on public transport. We can do it at work, at home, and anywhere in-between.

The very good news is that if you want to improve your ability to give skilled attention, and all subsequent communication skills, the world is your playground. And, like all other forms of training, the more you treat it as play – with the same curiosity, gratitude and joy that Sam walks in the park – the more quickly you will progress and the more you will want to keep learning.

Curiosity is important because it is the best of all antidotes to habitual thinking and habitual experiencing and, as we age, we risk becoming creatures of habit.

There are all sorts of good reasons why it makes sense to be habitual on a daily basis. There are also times in every day when we need to discard certain habits in favour of giving skilled attention.

These times include whenever we are communicating with others.

We can't listen properly through the incessant buzz of habit. We can't hear accurately what is being said, let alone what isn't being said, through the soundproofed wall of presumption; that's the wall we create every time we engage with another person, certain that we know who they are and what they have to say. It's the wall we lean against whenever we tell ourselves 'I've heard this all before' and retreat into our own head instead of finding new ways into theirs. It's the wall that blocks out forgetfulness, curiosity, awareness and respect, those essential ingredients for skilled and ethical communication.

How, then, do we create the ability to give such skilled attention that we hear not only what is said, but also what isn't; so that we recognise not just the words but also the (sometimes hidden) meaning;[16] so that we see the smallest, most fleeting expressions and gestures and recognise their message; so that we learn to see below the surface?

―――――――――――――――――――

[16] And if a man, albeit a genius, can listen to a scallop, we can all, surely, learn to listen to other human beings?

Paradoxically, we do it by developing the ability to forget. What do we need to forget? Thankfully, this I can remember. We need to forget our perception filters. We need to forget our attachment to own world view, temporarily, at least, in favour of exploring and understanding someone else's.

Forgetfulness, attention-giving and successful communication

Think of attention-giving as a beautiful sword. Actually, think of it as the very edge of that sword. To sharpen that edge, the swordsmith uses a stone to remove parts of the blade; the sharper the blade becomes, the less of it there is.

Similarly, the more we hold on to our sense of self and all associated perception filters, the more we blunt our attention. We literally lack the edge necessary to cut through the numerous, complex stimuli around us.

The lesson is:

In order to sharpen our attention, we have to let go of everything but our intention.[17]

We need to be comfortable not-knowing. We need to be at home moving into the uncertainty of human interaction, motivated purely by the need to achieve our ethically appropriate outcome. We need to forget all else for as long as it takes.

There are three reasons why that might appear easier said than done.

Firstly, because the human brain is working constantly to predict what's happening in our environment. Research is suggesting that our brain doesn't just passively receive and

---

[17]And, once we've set our intention, we can forget that, too. Our subconscious will look after it just fine.

classify information from our senses; rather it is continuously using that information to predict what is going to happen next and what behaviours and responses are most likely to be successful.

Through a process that some refer to as predictive coding, our brain adapts in response to experience, making increasingly detailed predictions when our expectations are met and, importantly, when they are not. Errors lead to new predictions, new learning and fundamental changes in our brain.

Writing more than 50 years ago W. Ross Ashby, the British psychiatrist and cyberneticist, stated:

'The whole function of the brain is summed up in: error correction.'

It seems that he was right. Our brain is working continually to determine the causes from the effects we experience, and so limit the degree of surprise or unpredictability we encounter as we go about our daily lives. Of course, much of the brain's predicting happens beyond our conscious awareness. It is only when thoughts about 'What does that mean?' or 'What might happen next?' begin to dominate that we lose our place in the communication flow.

Our goal therefore is to dampen down, disassociate from, or stop our thoughts whenever we need to communicate and converse with insight and precision. We can all learn how to do this. There are many different practices that improve our ability to be deliberately thoughtless and forgetful. I'm going to share eight of them in a moment.

Now, though, I'm going to highlight the benefits associated with this deliberate thoughtlessness. They are:

- Our sensory acuity increases significantly.
- Our understanding of others also increases.
- We are temporarily freed from our own issues.

The more we shed our perception filters and enter the flow of

Us, the more our own, personal concerns disappear. It's another way in which highly skilled, ethical communication creates win-win outcomes.

The second reason why creating this forgetful state doesn't necessarily seem easy to achieve, is because we are too-often taught that not-knowing is a state of weakness; that the conscious and deliberate acquisition and remembering of knowledge is the priority.

Throughout most of our education we are encouraged to know things and are praised and rewarded when we do. The message seems to be: know as much as possible as quickly as possible. Uncertainty, forgetfulness and not-knowing are rarely, if ever, identified or encouraged as desired learning states or as prized educational outcomes. And yet, if we are certain in our knowledge how can we ever be curious?

Now, just to be clear, I'm not suggesting that knowledge should be ignored in favour of forgetfulness and a well-meaning intention. This isn't an either-or situation.[18] I've already talked about the absolute importance of audience analysis and the role it plays in creating successful communication.

What I am saying is that, once we have done our deliberate analysis, we can entrust that knowledge to the silence and power of our subconscious, confident it will help guide our responses whenever we wish to create and enter the communication flow. And, of course, we can engage in another round of conscious analysis later, when the interaction is over, and we have feedback to consider.

The third reason why forgetting yourself can seem easier said than done, is because in many cultures people are encouraged, if not taught, to prioritise self over all else.

---

[18] Given what I've ready said about the transition from Me to You to Us, it would be contradictory to argue for a dualistic approach here.

The greatest ethical communicators don't do this. They cannot. It's impossible to gain heartfelt insight into someone else during the immediacy of an interaction if you are continually prioritising yourself. Simply put:

If you truly want to walk a mile in someone else's shoes, take your own shoes off first.

We can all do that.

We can all be deliberately forgetful if we have the desire to do so. And the good news is that, despite the three reasons I've just shared, we are all pretty good at forgetting. We do it frequently every day.

Admittedly there are times when our forgetfulness is unintended and unhelpful; equally, though, there are many occasions when it is the inevitable and necessary by-product of what we are experiencing in the here-and-now. For example, whenever we are concentrating on a specific task, or transported into a fictional realm by a novel, or looking at a person we love, we forget everything else – even if we don't mean to.

The type of forgetting that is an integral part of the communication flow is a far more deliberate activity. It's something we choose to do. It can be understood as:

The deliberate transference of something from the conscious to the subconscious mind.

It's the ability to do this deliberately that is so important when seeking to communicate powerfully, positively and ethically.

It's important because this temporary non-attachment to our own perception filters creates the freedom to communicate as never before. This is appropriate because every communication is unique. It has never been done before; it will never be done again.

René Descartes wrote his well-known phrase, 'Je pense, donc je suis', translated into Latin as 'Cogito ergo sum' and into

English as, 'I think therefore I am' in his 'Discourse on the Method' in 1637.

His emphasis on the importance of thinking, and the subsequent priority many people have given to that practice, has created a blind alley that limits our growth as communicators. Thinking is only one part of the communication process,[19] and it is a part we must be able to discard when necessary.

I can never read Descartes' quote without imagining an extra couple of words at the end, making it read: 'I think therefore I am. (I think.)'

Given that we feel emotions before we think, we could write a new version of Descartes's famous phrase, which would read:

'I feel emotion therefore I am.'

And if we want to define ourselves as social communicators, any of these would do:

'I hear silence therefore I hear you clearly.'
'I avoid giving a casual glance therefore I see you.'
'I am curious therefore I learn.'
'I forget therefore I am free to understand you.'

However, freedom without focus is equally inappropriate.

Remember, every communication creates an outcome. This is inevitable. Remember, too, that the outcome is emotional first, followed – often very swiftly – by rational thinking, analysis and/or decision-making. That's why we need to establish with absolute clarity the outcome we desire to achieve.

Think of this as your outcome goal. It's the target you are aiming for, the ultimate purpose of your unique

---

[19] It's only one part of being human. (That's why it's only one part of the communication process.)

communication.

Non-attachment gives you the freedom to achieve and, when appropriate, develop your outcome goal. It also frees you to identify and then meet the communication needs of those you are seeking to influence, by interacting in the most necessary and creative of ways. Think of these ways as your process goals. Ironically, and wonderfully, non-attachment also frees us from building an unbreakable commitment to our process goals (and, occasionally, even our outcome goal). It does this because non-attachment helps to make us super-receptive to feedback. And if the feedback shows us that something isn't working, or that there is a better way, non-attachment makes adapting easy.

That's why, in the most successful communication(s), we achieve our process goals en route to achieving our outcome goal by creating a uniquely interactive feedback loop.

With that said, let's turn to some practical approaches.

Here are the promised eight practices that will help you to forget your perception filters, move away from the noise of your own life, and focus on the other whilst giving skilled attention:

- Diaphragmatic breathing.
- Meditation.
- Becoming the editor of our own thoughts.
- Opening the curtains.
- Using nature and/or art.
- Surrendering to our subconscious.
- Fishing.
- Focusing on someone else.

Diaphragmatic breathing

a) How do we do it?

Begin by relaxing your shoulders, your hands and your

stomach. Then breathe in gently and deeply, extending your lower stomach as you do, imagining the breath going all the way down to the point about 2 centimetres below your belly button.

Hold the breath there for a couple of seconds before exhaling through your nose whilst gently contracting your stomach. As you exhale let your shoulders and the rest of your body relax even more. Perform in sets of 4 breaths as required.

If you need to energise yourself, again relax your body first and then breathe strongly and deeply in through your nose raising your chest as much as you can, filling your lungs with air. Breathe out equally forcefully, this time through your mouth. Again, perform in sets of 4.

You can do these breathing exercises either sitting, standing or laying down.

b) What are the benefits?

They are many and varied. Some research suggests regular diaphragmatic breathing contributes to emotional balance and social adaption. Whilst other research concludes that it helps to reduce stress (by decreasing cortisol release), lowers the heart rate and also helps to lower blood pressure.

In other words, it enhances our ability to give skilled attention in a calm, focused manner.

Meditation

a) How do we do it?

Before I identify some of the many ways to meditate, let me first explain what is meant by 'meditation'. Whilst there is no universally accepted definition, we can regard it here as a focusing of the mind on a specific stimulus, to develop awareness and attention-giving, and achieve a calm, emotional mental state.

For example, you can focus exclusively on a single object such as a flower or a candle flame, or even your own reflection. You can listen to a sound, or a piece of music, or repeat a specific mantra. You can focus on your breath, whether that is how you breathe naturally or the deliberate diaphragmatic breathing I've just outlined.

You can also meditate by spending time quietly observing your thoughts – letting them happen – rather than automatically engaging with them. You can do this in a variety of ways. For example, you might visualise your thoughts as if they are written in a book that you can close whenever you want to end that particular thought process. Or you might imagine thoughts as clouds, travelling across the sky before disappearing from view. The goal, though, is always the same: to create a sense of space, of distance, between yourself and your thoughts.

Depending on the method of meditation you choose, you can practise whilst sitting, standing, lying or moving.

You can also meditate at any time.

Personally, I experience the benefits of meditation most fully by incorporating it at the beginning and at the end of my day. First thing in the morning, it helps to set the state for everything that is to follow. As the final part of my preparing-to-sleep routine, it helps calm and relax my mind and body.

If you have never meditated before and decide to give it a go, I'd recommend experimenting to find the method that works best for you – begin with the one that instinctively appeals the most – and then sandwich the activities and experiences of each day between a minimum of 5 and a maximum of 15 minutes meditation.

b) What are the benefits?

Research suggests that regular meditation lengthens our attention span and increases awareness. It also quietens activity in the medial prefrontal cortex, an area of the brain that is activated whenever we are having thoughts about ourselves.

According to Dr John Sullivan, a leading American Clinical and Sports Psychologist:

'The ultimate goal of meditation is to slow down the cognitive processing of our conscious brain. This in turn slows both heart rate and stomach activity, whilst also reducing the vagus nerve reaction. The result is an increased ability to control our attention-giving and emotional responses.'

Silence and meditation, then, can be used to create the foundation for skilled attention-giving and insightful communication.

Becoming the editor of our own thoughts

a) How do we do it?

By treating our thoughts as if they are words we are producing on a screen or a page, seeing or hearing them (or both) from the constructively critical perspective of a friendly editor.

The difference between this and observing our thoughts whilst meditating, is that, in this activity, we have the permission and the power to edit our thoughts to ensure they serve the most useful purpose. It's important to be a friendly, supportive and compassionate editor throughout. Avoid judging any thought in a negative manner. Rather just observe and acknowledge it, consider if it's fit for purpose and, if not, edit accordingly.

Arguably, the most powerful edit we can make is to take the word 'I' (or 'Me', 'Mine', 'Myself' and any other equivalent) out of our thoughts.

The reason is because thoughts filled with 'I' keep a person locked into the Me part of the Me – You – Us triumvirate. These thoughts limit the ability to focus clearly on the other and prevent any chance of creating and entering into the flow of Us.

As your own thought-editor, every time you think the word 'I' change it to your preferred personal pronoun. Or change the structure of the entire thought to avoid any direct reference to yourself.

For example, the thought, 'I can't concentrate on writing this email, because I'm so unsure about how the upcoming meeting is going to go,' can be edited to:

'She/He/They wouldn't concentrate on writing her/his/their email, because her/his/their brain was trying to predict a future outcome.'

Note this example includes three other powerful thought-edits:

- The original word 'can't' has been edited to 'wouldn't'. The former implying hopelessness, the latter acknowledging choice.
- The underlying sense of uncertainty was reframed as an understandable brain function.
- The past tense was used, implying that the lack of concentration had ended.

If you want to use this practice, adopt a 'little and often' approach. Start out monitoring and editing your thoughts for just two or three minutes at a time, several times a day, ideally when you are in-between activities or conversations.

This is precisely the time when the brain's default mode network will most obviously activate, encouraging your thoughts to turn towards others and the social interactions you have had, or might have, with them.

Practise by editing your thoughts as suggested above and, if you are also visualising a future interaction, focus your mind's eye on the other person/people or on the interaction between you, rather than just on yourself.

b) What are the benefits?

Successful thought-editing influences our emotional states positively, enhances our ability to forget any unhelpful perception filters and so sharpens our attention, increasing the likelihood of a magical communication flow.

Opening the curtains.

a) How do we do it?

It's easy. When you wake up in the morning, get out of bed, open the curtains and look out of the window.[20]
Oh! The most important thing – you must forget what the view is before you open the curtains. I realise that it's a view you have probably seen countless times, and that you might even start thinking about the view before you start looking. Regardless, the challenge, and the value of the activity, is still the same. It's an exercise in forgetting. It's an exercise in letting go of what you think you know, so you see what is there as if for the first time.
Of course, you don't just need your bedroom curtains and window to practise this. The world is filled with opportunities. Over time you might even learn to treat your eyes as metaphorical curtains, with every blink bringing a new reveal and a new chance to gain a fresh perspective.

b) What are the benefits?

Increased sensory acuity and the joy of newness and insight.

Using nature and/or art.

a) How do we do it?

This is a development of opening the curtains. It's practice in experiencing something as if never before. Sam does it every time we walk in the park.[21] We can do it by truly committing ourselves to seeing, hearing, smelling, tasting and feeling as if

---

[20] Make sure you put some clothes on first.
[21] I do my best to follow his lead.

50

for the first time whenever we engage with nature in all its forms, and whenever we engage with art in all its forms.

Both nature and art encourage us to let go, to submit and sense both our connection and the insight that springs from this.

There is a world of difference between passing through a park, a forest, or an art gallery, and being present whilst there.

When passing through, we simply treat what is around us as objects that we are moving by; much as we treat the landscape when driving quickly along a motorway, or the views of other people when we are keen to promote our own perspective.

When we submit to being fully present, we let go of the personal perception filters that prevent us from connecting with others. We are then more likely to experience the deep, rather than the surface, structure that exists.

Not surprisingly, we access this state by forgetting everything that creates our usual expectations and interpretations. We can do this by using any of the other methods highlighted here. Or by giving nature and art permission to challenge, change, broaden, deepen, or even transform our world view and the associated sense of who we are.

After all, we are not distinct from nature, we are an integral and powerful aspect of it. And, because all forms of art are created by people seeking to express their ideas and/or experiences, we can treat art with the same respect, curiosity and desire for understanding that we would treat the artist.

And we don't just have to look at someone else's art, we can create our own.

Whilst we can meditate by looking at an object, we can make it a more active meditation by drawing what we see.[22]

------

[22] Drawing what we see is very different from drawing an interpretation, or drawing what we imagine. The greatest artists see deep structure, not just surface structure.

A final point here: nature is everywhere, from our garden to the sky and beyond; art is everywhere, too. I said earlier that all forms of art are forms of communication. Artists, like nature, offer themselves to us. We all grow if we learn how to cross the communication synapse successfully and experience the connection this creates.

b) What are the benefits?

Connectivity and rapport.
A sense of separation can foster disinterest, discord, dislike and/or defiance. Whilst there are times when we might need to communicate our differences – sometimes profoundly so – the starting point for successful communication is understanding, and a willingness and ability to create relationships that are appropriate and mutually beneficial.

Surrendering to our subconscious.

a) How do we do it?

By consciously accepting that our subconscious has authority and can be trusted.
There is much research suggesting that the majority of human processing is done beyond our conscious awareness. Indeed, we learn skills with the aim of becoming unconsciously competent.
Surrendering to our subconscious is at the core of appropriate forgetfulness. We can therefore trust our subconscious to help us create, and operate within, the communication flow.
I'm referring to it as surrendering because we cannot consciously engage with our subconscious in real-time. We can only dampen down the activity of the conscious mind to let the subconscious take the lead.
The breathing and meditation practices I discussed earlier both help us to achieve this. So does acknowledging the importance of the subconscious repeatedly throughout the

day; recognising its presence and essential role in our existence.

You might, for example, do it every morning when you wake and last thing at night when you go to bed – after all none of us consciously keep our bodies functioning whilst we sleep.

It's also easier to surrender to your subconscious if you're well trained and well prepared. That's as true for communication as it is for sport and any other line of work. If we keep studying, developing and applying our skills, reviewing and learning from feedback, and if we've also had time to undertake audience analysis, the conscious mind is more easily bypassed.

b) What are the benefits?

Rapport and influence.

When insights from the subconscious guide our words and actions, Me and You both disappear within the flow of Us.

Fishing

a) How do we do it?

Choose your bait appropriately, cast it out, then sit back and watch what happens. The bait in this case are words, phrases, stories, questions, ideas, or points of view.

Simply say something that is relevant, or at least tangential, to the conversation and observe how the other(s) respond.

The key word here is 'observe'. Whenever we become too caught up in the importance of our own words, we stop giving skilled attention to the person, or people, we are talking to.

So, when we go fishing, we assume the role of an observer; present and alert, recognising feedback accurately and learning from it. We can then use our next comments to test how accurately we have identified the other person's current state. Once we are sure we understand them sufficiently, we can move on.

Sometimes when I go fishing, I'll share unexpected

information; sometimes I'll offer a particular point of view, use specific language, ask a question, or repeat a story. In different ways, these all help reveal the other person's preferred communication patterns, current state, values, limitations and/or agenda.

b) What are the benefits?

Fishing plays a useful role in audience analysis, providing insights that enable a shift in the communication flow. It also reminds us that words are sounds and symbols that fulfil functions.

Focusing on someone else

a) How do we do it?

Just spend a minute or two several times a day focusing solely on another person. They don't have to be with, or near, you at the time. (Although they can be.) You don't need to know them very well. (Although you might.) Just forget yourself and focus as completely as possible on the other. The aim is to do so without:

- Assigning value judgments.
- Considering their impact in your life.

In other words, focus on the person and not the relationship they share with you; delete any sense of yourself as you focus on the other.

b) What are the benefits?

An increased willingness and ability to forget oneself in favour of another. This, in turn, helps the transition from Me to You to Us.

Talking of transition, it's time now to transition from these eight practices for great state creation, to the importance of Listening and Looking. We'll address them in that order.

Listening

I'm going to begin by making a claim that might surprise you. It's this:

Of all the interpersonal communication skills listening is the most important.

Why do I say this?

Because listening is the ability to recognise accurately the messages someone else is sharing.

Active listening is the act of hearing what is not said as clearly as what is. It is the ability to hear beyond the surface noise and identify the insights and truths that are being revealed. Indeed, at its very best, active listening is a combination of attitudes and skills applied for the sole purpose of understanding another human being. That is why it is at the heart of skilled attention-giving.

Let me take a minute to tell you a quick story about the greatest listener I've ever known:

His name is Pete. He was twenty-eight years old when we first met at the local public baths where, once a week, I taught swimming to people with various disabilities. Pete had been blind since birth.

Pete and I spent most of our time together in the water. This is important because it makes the next part of the story even more incredible.

One bright, sunny morning I parked my car as near to a Post Office as I could and walked inside intending to post a small package. The queue stretched from the counter to the open door. There were probably seven people ahead of me. Some of them were talking to each other. Those at the counter were talking to the people serving them. I stood silently at the rear of the queue.

Suddenly, without saying a word, Pete stepped out of the line. He was almost at the counter. I hadn't seen him. He turned, looked pointedly in my direction, and smiled a greeting.

'Pete!' I said. 'How are you? And how the heck did you know I was here?'

His smile broadened. 'I'm very well, thank you,' he said. 'And I knew you were here because I heard your footsteps as you approached the door...'

Now, my experience has been that when people lose one sense, their other senses sharpen to compensate. So, I'm not suggesting that those of us who are fortunate enough to see and hear, can necessarily develop their listening to match Pete's. I am saying, though, that we should avoid taking our senses for granted and work constantly to improve them.

Our starting point is understanding that:

- Listening is a skill.
- As with every other skill it is dependent on the development of a range of attributes and an underpinning attitude.
- The level and value of our interpersonal communication is determined by the clarity with which we listen.

I've already identified what I consider to be the most important attributes, and shared some ways you can develop them.

And you already know what the underpinning attitude is: it's the desire to really understand the person with whom we are communicating; to be able to see things from their perspective, to hear the real messages they are sharing, to recognise their emotions.

Listening is best understood, therefore, as a multi-sensory, all-encompassing activity that incorporates looking and feeling. It is total absorption in the other. It is dependent upon the ability to silence external and internal noise.

The one-liner is:

Silence really is golden if you want to be a great listener.

Sam is a great listener. He's also frequently silent. He spends most of his life in silence. He makes it look easy. But then, experts always do.

Over the years, I've done my best to follow his example. In doing so, I've come to appreciate that silence is an integral part of communication, and that there are, essentially, three types of silence. These are:

- Silence of the mouth.
- Silence of the mind.
- Silence beyond our conscious control.

Silence of the mouth is achieved by talking less. It's really that simple. Well, it's that simple to write. It can be a tad more challenging to put into practice. That's because it's too easy to prioritise saying whatever it is we have to say, rather than prioritising listening to whatever it is the other person has to say.

Silence of the mouth is achieved by listening first, listening second and listening third, before deciding whether or not to speak. Even if we are asked to give a public talk, the same principle applies. Listen carefully to what the audience needs; only when we really understand that, can we decide if we will be a congruent messenger, capable of providing a worthwhile talk.

Silence of the mind is achieved by managing, limiting and/or stopping thoughts. Words that come from a silent mind tend to be delivered differently and have a different effect to words that rush from a busy mind.

The silence that exists beyond our conscious control is a permanent, all-pervading silence. This silence is not the opposite of sound. It is the home of sound; if sound travels in waves, this silence is the ocean providing the energy and direction.

You can practise listening to this silence.

The process is easy: just relax and give yourself permission to hear it. Put a metaphorical loving arm around your conscious mind if it tries to tell you that, by definition, it's not possible to hear silence and just listen.[23] If you persevere, you might well find that, listening to silence changes how you hear so-called sounds.

Many of the eight practices identified previously will help you to recognise and be comfortable within the three types of silence and, therefore, to listen with greater acuity.

You can also use music to develop your listening. The key is to avoid having music playing as background noise and, instead, to listen to the rhythms, shifts and changes in tempo. If there is a singer, ignore the meaning of their words and listen to them as if they are musical notes – just part of the overall sound.

Phone conversations also provide ideal training opportunities. As Pete's story highlights, whenever we can't see someone, we are forced to listen more acutely. Whatever training methods we adopt, we need to be deliberate in our training because:

a) In our busy, daily schedules it's very easy to rush from one interaction to the next without taking even a moment or two to attend to our own state. Too often we carry the noise from the conversation we have just left with us into the next conversation. And we might repeat this several times a day, creating a level of internal noise that makes it all-but impossible to hear clearly what people are sharing with us here and now.

Simply put, we cannot hear with clarity if we are creating and carrying around a build-up of sound inside our mind.

---

[23] What's that I hear you ask? – What does silence sound like? Ok. I'll tell you. It sounds like a smile...

b) We too often ignore signs of personal fatigue and push on regardless believing:

- This is a sign of professionalism.
- The quality of our performance won't be damaged.

We're wrong on both counts. With listening, as with any other activity you wish to excel at, rest and recovery is as important as practising the skill. To have the sensory acuity necessary to be a great listener we need the energy to be alert. After all, in many situations we'll not only be listening, we'll also be looking.

Looking

It is, of course, possible to look without seeing accurately, just as it's possible to listen without hearing clearly.
Our goal is to look so that we gain insight.
So, without further ado, cast your eyes over the diagram below and answer the question, 'How many triangles are there?'

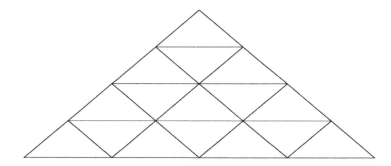

I wonder for how long you gave your attention to the task, and what answer you arrived at?
One thing I do know for sure is that you cannot solve the problem accurately if you give it only a casual glance. Therein lies the challenge.

We cannot gain accurate insights into those with whom we are communicating if we offer them only a casual glance. And it's all too easy to give people, places and situations, nothing more than that, even when we mean to be attentive.

There are several reasons why:

Firstly, few of us have been trained rigorously and well in how to achieve insight. Just because our eyes are healthy doesn't mean that we know how to see insightfully, and it certainly doesn't mean that we know how to see constantly and consistently. Like every other skill, seeing requires a progressive training methodology and a willingness to practise. Stamina is developed over time.

Secondly, we are being bombarded constantly by a mass of stimuli. We manage this by deleting, distorting and generalising much of what we experience. This can lead us into accepting the first obvious answer or interpretation, confident that we have understood accurately what is going on around us.

Thirdly, our perception filters will blinker us if we let them. They make it easy for us to delete, distort and generalise in particular ways.

The final reason for using only a casual glance is familiarity. Unless managed deliberately and with great care, familiarity deafens and blinds.

In The Introduction I wrote about the importance of respect and understanding. I wrote it in that order because respect precedes understanding. Our word 'respect' comes from the Latin *respectere*, meaning to *look back* and *consider*, and from the Middle French word *respecter* meaning to *notice with special attention*.

You can't offer a casual glance and be respectful. If you truly want to show respect, you must look deeply and accurately. So, how can we develop our visual acuity?

Three interconnected ways are:

- By using our peripheral vision deliberately and often.
- By looking at space rather than objects.
- By being silent when we look.

Peripheral vision is the part of our vision that is outside the centre of our gaze.

Our visual field is normally approximately 170 degrees around. Peripheral vision comprises 100 of those degrees. Yet, despite its prominence, most of us tend to be unaware of it. My experience is that the more we deliberately use our peripheral vision, the more easily we observe and the more accurately we identify.

Here's one way we can use our peripheral vision:

When engaging in face-to-face communication, rather than directing your vision onto the physicality of the other person – their eyes, their face, their body – look instead over and beyond their shoulders and into the wider environment. (The person will still feel as if you are looking at them naturally.)

Then just let your peripheral vision focus on the space rather than the people or any objects that are present within it. You will, of course, still see who or what is there – just from a different perspective.

What should we be thinking as we look beyond their shoulders?

Ideally, nothing at all. Be silent, freed from those perception filters that encourage a casual glance. You see, just as the most irresistible words grow out of silence, so does the most perceptive visual acuity. And if you're still wondering how many triangles there are in the diagram, I urge you to look for yourself.

The answer is insight.

Attitudes, attributes and a second definition

In closing this chapter, I'd like to:

- Highlight the relationship between attitudes, attributes and space.
- Introduce the third and fourth 'A's without which attitudes and attributes are pointless.
- Share my second definition of communication.

Here they are:

Attitudes are what we develop within ourselves, within our internal space. Attributes are what we develop in order to manage, and move through, our external space. Attitudes are the foundation, the springboard, from which we manifest our attributes; the quality of our performance as communicators and, indeed, in every other way, is linked inescapably to the appropriateness of our attitude.

Our third 'A' is Action. The reason for developing Attitudes and Attributes is so that we can take Action.

Whilst communication, and the influence created by it, can be obvious or subtle, it is always active. I mentioned earlier that there are no passive words, that's because all forms of communication are, inevitably, forms of action. Listening so that we hear, looking so that we see and speaking so that we influence as intended are actions of the greatest significance.

To do these well we need our fourth 'A', which is Adaptability. Not only do we need to be willing and able to use the communication patterns of others (and I'll talk a lot more about those shortly) we also need to adapt in response to unexpected feedback. To achieve this adaptability, we must be free from any expectations, preconceptions or, indeed, any sense of how well (or not) the communication is progressing. In my experience, we adapt best in response to feedback, when we are fully present in the moment and focused as completely as possible on the other.

When we combine the most appropriate attitudes with the best attributes and adaptability, we can connect with others, and influence ethically and elegantly.

That's why our second definition of communication reads:

Communication is how we share our presence through space.

'I make my presence known every time someone comes to our door. When it's Chris returning home, even if he's only been gone for a couple of minutes, I can barely control my joy.'

Chapter Two

Being a Skilled Communicator (ii)

The principles, processes and models that enable us to harness and use the power of conversations.

Principles

These are:

- Go first!
- Congruency creates authority.
- Create the state then operate.
- Set positive outcomes.
- The meaning of communication is the response you get.
- There is no failure only feedback.
- People do things for their reasons, not ours.
- People respond to their experience, not reality.
- Influence is inevitable.
- Tell stories.
- Know when to focus on the big picture; know when to focus on detail.
- Be curious enough to ask questions – and be great at asking and answering questions.
- Words travel on the breath.

Go first!

The principle of going first, of starting before it starts, incorporates the following elements: continual study and development of our communication skills and associated attitudes and attributes; establishing clearly defined outcomes; audience analysis; creating the state before we operate; leading the communication as soon as it is appropriate to do so.

The most successful communicators always go first. It's the most obvious sign of their commitment to their cause. Sam never waits; he always takes the initiative. Which is not to say that he rushes in. Sometimes he's very subtle in his approach.[24] His lesson is: going first isn't always an obvious thing. And there are many occasions when it's appropriate for it to be unnoticed. Sometimes our influence is most powerful when, in a seemingly magical sense, it's operating below the conscious awareness of others.

In this regard, there are several important differences between a Communication Magician and a stage magician.

Firstly, stage magicians only ever have one desired outcome: to entertain their audience. Communication Magicians seek to create different outcomes in different contexts.

Secondly, we know whenever a stage magician is performing a trick, we just can't see how they are doing it. Whereas, the best Communication Magicians will sometimes choose to weave their magic, and achieve their goal, unnoticed.

Thirdly, when seeking to create influence, Communication Magicians are likely to experience any of the following responses:

- Support (maybe even gratitude).
- Apathy.
- Resistance.

This is as true when explaining to a child why their behaviour must change, as it is when seeking to introduce a new business strategy or leading a campaign to win an election.

The bottom line is, we always need permission from others to achieve our goals. If we go first, if we start before others realise that we have, we are automatically several steps ahead in the

---

[24] As he demonstrates in the final story in the book.

influencing process.

Congruency creates authority

It's a common tendency to judge the value of the message by the perceived qualities of the messenger. It's essential, therefore, that we are regarded as a reliable and trustworthy messenger. Ideally, our audience needs to acknowledge us as the most appropriate communicator on the given topic.

Four ways we can achieve this are:

- To have demonstrable expertise.
- To communicate skilfully, creating rapport and making knowledge accessible.
- To demonstrate our values and associated ethical stance through our actions as well as our words.
- To make clear the deep-rooted motivation that is compelling us to communicate and influence.

This motivation is the cause that I mentioned earlier. It's the emotional compulsion that drives us to influence. As an emotional compulsion it exists within us. We can feel it, in our stomach or our chest, or both, or elsewhere, if we pause and explore.

This isn't just a matter of self-reflection, but also of delivery. For example, a purely intellectual point of view is likely to be expressed very differently from one that is heart-felt. Whilst words that spring from a life-long commitment are likely to be different from those sparked by a relatively recent discovery.

Whenever we exercise the emotional compulsion within us, our words take on an even greater power; engaging and moving those who receive them.

Create the state then operate

To be a successful communicator there are two internal states we must manage.

These are:

- Our own.
- Those of the people with whom we are communicating.

Not surprisingly, we'll begin by focusing on our own state. Beyond the methods I've already discussed, here's an additional technique we can use to manage our own state. It's called:

Reframing.

Reframing is the ability to change the frame of reference through which we perceive an experience or interpret a message. Reframing encourages a change of perspective.

If you have ever had a picture that needed framing, you know what a difference the frame makes. If you have a great picture and surround it with an inappropriate frame, the picture invariably suffers. Likewise, a great frame can make a quite ordinary picture far more appealing.

We can choose how we frame and, therefore, view our experiences, just as we can choose how we frame pictures.

There are, essentially, two types of reframe. These are:

- Context reframing.
- Content reframing.

Context reframing involves taking a behaviour that appears undesirable and exploring how it might be useful in a different context.

Many children's stories and fairy tales incorporate context reframing. For example, Rudolph the Red-Nosed Reindeer was ridiculed because of the brightness of his nose until that same brightness lit the way home on a dark and dangerous winter's night.

Content reframing involves changing the meaning of a situation by changing the way you see, hear or represent it. Here's an example:

A businessman spent some time moaning to me about the fact that he had paid far more income tax than in previous years. As we talked, he came to appreciate that his increased tax bill was a direct result of his increased success. Instead of crying into his beer, he bought a bottle of champagne to toast his achievement. He had successfully reframed his experience and changed his state.

When it comes to managing the state of those with whom you are communicating, aim to move them into the most receptive, action-ready state before addressing the issue that has brought you together.

Surgeons always ensure their patients are suitably prepared before asking for a scalpel, great salesmen and women do the same before asking someone to part with their money.[25] Whenever we are aiming to influence another human being, we use the power of conversations to lay the groundwork. The more we create the desired state in the other person, or people, the more readily they will join in the direction of our flow.

Once this is achieved, the aim is to keep them in the most appropriate state for the rest of the interaction.

And we can use our own state, not just our words and gestures, to influence the state of others. That's because influence is inevitable, and states are contagious.

I first learnt that in the late 1970's when I began working as a teacher of Religious Education in inner-city comprehensive schools. It wasn't a job for the faint-hearted. Many of the children I worked with looked at RE and Music teachers in exactly the same way that hungry lions look at the weakest zebra in the herd.

To be an effective teacher in such a situation – heck, just as a matter of survival – you had to create an appropriate state

------

[25] They don't use drugs or scalpels, obviously.

before you operated. That meant ensuring you felt more like the king of the jungle than a three-legged zebra.

With regard to managing the children's states, it started before they even came into the classroom. It started in the corridors. If you've ever wondered why teachers might require pupils to line up quietly outside the room, it's because they are creating appropriate, action-ready states.

If, for example, I wanted children to be calm at the start of my lesson, I created that state in the corridor. If I wanted them to be excited, I simply changed the nature of our interaction.

Interestingly, years later, having worked as a senior manager, a management trainer, business consultant and university lecturer, I came to appreciate the importance of conversations in corridors, no matter what the organisation.

In those brief exchanges, information can be shared, states can be enhanced or changed, and the seeds of influence can be sown.

Set positive outcomes

This is a development of the point I've made already about the need for clearly defined outcomes: ensure they are stated positively.

A positive outcome identifies what is to be achieved or gained. A negative outcome identifies only what is to be stopped or avoided.

Examples of negative outcomes are:

- 'My intention is to stop him interrupting others in meetings.'
- 'I'm studying for an MBA because it's one way of ensuring that my career prospects are not limited.'
- 'I'm retiring at fifty-five, because I want to be sure I don't work myself into an early grave.'

If these were to be restated as positive outcomes, they might be:

- 'I want him to listen, silently and respectfully, to the other committee members.'
- 'I'm studying for an MBA because I want to develop my knowledge and skill base and be a Director by the time I'm thirty.'
- 'I'm retiring at fifty-five, because I want to spend as much time as possible travelling the world.'

When we set positive outcomes, we:

- Establish clear, measurable goals we can work towards.
- Make clear what success looks like.
- Create a vision of a valuable, new future.

The meaning of communication is the response you get

This simply means taking responsibility for ensuring that your message is understood in precisely the way you intended.

If the other person doesn't understand or misinterprets what you've said, have the willingness and mental flexibility to present the message differently until you do achieve your desired outcome.

The next time you hear someone say, 'I just don't know what the matter is with him. He doesn't understand what I'm saying...' be reminded of your personal responsibility for delivering messages in the style and manner most suited to your audience.

Sam has never chased our postman. I think it's because he appreciates the fact that he delivers messages to the right place, at the right time, in the right way.

There is no failure only feedback

This is a powerful reframe. And, just like deliberate forgetfulness, it can seem easier said than done.

When feedback reveals that our words are being ignored,

rejected, or attacked, it's all-too easy for us to feel the pain of social rejection, and/or the tightening of negative beliefs and associated self-doubt.

The ability to give skilled attention, to forget Me in favour of You and then Us, inhibits such a response. This, in turn, enables us to access the space through which we can recognise feedback for what it is:

Feedback is the gift of informative energy.

It's an energy sourced by our communication. And, as with all energy, we can choose to:

- Challenge and/or block it.
- Encourage it as it is.
- Harness and redirect it.

Feedback is an integral part of the inevitable and necessary flow of interconnectivity. All feedback offers:

- Insights into the provider.
- Opportunities for us to learn about our own performance.
- The chance to practise emotional management.

One thing that helped me become used to feedback, and learn how to use it, was the realisation that feedback is happening all the time.

Everywhere we go, no matter what we do, our brain is continually analysing the environment, responding to stimuli, processing and predicting, providing feedback. Sometimes we are aware of this and often we're not. Regardless, it's happening every moment of every day. Everyone around us is doing it, too.

Not only are we receiving feedback from others and our environment, we are also giving ourselves feedback continually. That's one very important reason why we need to be aware of, and manage, our own emotional and physical state(s) as a precursor to communicating skilfully and elegantly. Feedback flows through and influences systems just as blood flows through a body influencing it. The mistake we make is regarding feedback as an occasional response, as something we choose to ask for, or that someone else chooses to offer. In reality, feedback is an ever-present source of learning. It can also be a great reminder that:

People do things for their reasons, not ours

The greatest influencers understand this and base their communication on it.

Some years ago, I was lucky enough to write a book about Diego Masciaga, then a Director and the Restaurant Manager of the world-famous 3 Michelin starred restaurant, The Waterside Inn. Diego was acknowledged globally as the master of customer service. The book was a study of his approach to customer service excellence.

Diego understood completely that every guest was there for their own reasons, and that those reasons had to be understood and catered for. I wrote:[26]

'From Diego's perspective every table in the restaurant is an individual world. The guests at each table are there for their own reasons and have their own expectations of what constitutes great Service. On top of this, their mood might also change as the hours pass. This means that the front-of-house staff have only a few paces – the space between tables – to shift their focus fully from one world to the next, to assess whether or not it is appropriate to speak whilst serving, to remember what they last talked about, or to remind themselves of

---

[26] Parker, C. The Diego Masciaga Way. Lessons From The Master Of Customer Service. 2014. Urbane Publications.

anything Diego might have said at the pre-briefing about the guests they are approaching.'

We don't have to work in a restaurant to realise and remember that people inevitably have their own reasons, even for doing the same things. The more we understand other people's motives, the more successfully we can communicate, creating positive emotions and improving the quality of their experience.

Which leads us to the next principle:

People interpret their experiences and treat these interpretations as reality

Last Sunday, I was watching a game of football in the park. At one point I saw a perfectly good tackle. The man next to me saw a foul warranting a yellow card. Sam the dog just watched a ball that needed chasing. We were all involved in the same event, and we all experienced it differently.

Why?

Perhaps because of the degree of attention we were giving to that particular incident. Or because of the relationships we shared with certain players. Or because of our beliefs and values.

No two people experience the world in exactly the same way. We interpret our experiences and assign meanings to them based on our perception filters, agendas, motivation and time available. The more we understand someone's interpretation of their experience, their emotional response to that, and the stories they are consequently telling themselves, the more opportunity we have to communicate with them in ways that enable us to influence as intended.

Influence is inevitable

I've already made the point that every time we interact, we influence. That's because words, gestures and expressions affect the human brain, and the brain affects emotions, attitudes and behaviours. That's why influence is inevitable. Therein lies our responsibility and our challenge. Whether or not we want to be, and whether or not we realise it, we are powerful influencers already.

Therefore, we could reasonably ask ourselves:

- How good do I need to be at influencing as intended?
- How frequently do I need to do this?

Now, as I've already made clear, I'm not suggesting that we can become perfect communicators, and I'm sure that we don't need to be anywhere near perfect to communicate so positively and powerfully that we make a significant difference to ourselves and those around us. And, given that there is no failure only feedback, our imperfections provide continual opportunities for us to learn and improve.

Here's a simple story that highlights some of my own imperfections, the inevitability of influence, and why Sam is my guru:

I came home from work one day feeling irritated and tired. There had been a number of pressing issues I'd had to manage, and I'd worked my communication skills to their limit.

By the time I'd taken my jacket off, Sam had his lead in his mouth and was bashing my shins with his head. I ignored him twice and, when he persisted, I shouted at him angrily. Sam dropped his lead and ran, quivering, into his basket.

It was not my finest hour. I'd made the mistake of thinking that I had finished influencing for the day. Here I was, at home, creating states in a negative way. I picked up Sam's lead, put my jacket back on, and asked his forgiveness. Sam is so strong he can carry anything apart from a grudge.

We had a great walk.

Tell stories

Stories are our oldest form of communication and influence. Stories were mimed or danced around a campfire. Stories were passed on from one generation to the next. And they still are. We continue to tell stories that teach as much as they entertain. Stories that introduce something new or remind us of universal truths. Stories that motivate, move and inspire.

We remember stories because they appeal to our brain's innate capability to create associations and meanings, to find connections between people and events. Stories are more memorable than facts alone because they are multi-sensory in nature and because they stimulate our imagination and emotions.

Stories can be told in seconds or hours. The most influential always engage the audience. They are about experiences, events, people, challenges, hopes and beliefs that the audience can relate to. They are told in language the audience understands.

Stories have played and continue to play a vital role in every country and every culture on the planet. They are at the core of what makes us human, which is why they are an essential part of creating influence.

In our modern world, there are two objects we can use to remind ourselves of the need to always start our stories brilliantly, and of the challenges we face in attracting and then keeping the attention of our audience.

These objects are the mobile phone and the remote control for the television. Consider how easy they make it for us all to move from one story to the next; how quickly we can lose interest and transfer, in a split-second, onto something else.

So, whenever you have a story to tell, imagine your audience holding a mobile phone or a remote control in their hands. If your story does not start brilliantly, they will turn to something else in an instant. If your story fails to maintain and develop their interest, they will do the same. In one sense, the mobile phone and the remote control throw down the greatest of challenges to every storyteller. The challenge is to:

Begin brilliantly and then get even better, because there is a world of stories out there, all just one second away.

Know when to focus on the big picture; know when to focus on detail

They both have their time and place. It's important we get them right.

Big picture focus is essential:

- When planning for future success.
- When needing to identify the implications of a change we are about to make.

Successful future planning is dependent on the creation of a clear and detailed vision to work towards. Clarity and appropriateness of this vision require both big picture strategic awareness and a bold, well-managed imagination.

When planning to introduce a change we can also use big picture focus as an ecology check, by which I mean identifying the knock-on effects of our actions on the people and environment(s) within which we are operating, and ensuring these effects are positive.

Focusing on detail is essential:

- For ensuring the quality of both process and outcome.
- For improving performance and avoiding errors.

And a focus on detail is also invaluable in helping us to manage difficult, or stressful, situations.

Under pressure we can use attention to detail to shrink our world down into small steps or easy-to-reach goals; directing our attention to the nearest target and focusing on how best to reach it, rather than being swamped by the apparent magnitude of the big picture.

Be curious enough to ask questions – and be great at asking and answering questions

I said earlier that every communication provides learning. Well, that's only true, of course, if we are seeking to learn. Curiosity is the vehicle that takes us on that journey of exploration. If we are not truly curious about others, we are going nowhere. And let's be clear, there's a world of difference between being genuinely curious about someone because we are committed to developing our relationship and creating some form of positive transformation, and simply prying into their lives.

Our word 'curious' comes from the Latin *curiosus*, which meant 'careful', 'diligent', 'inquiring eagerly'. When learning about someone else, we need to do so carefully and diligently, respecting their boundaries and values, whilst ensuring that our interpretations and findings are accurate. We need to do so eagerly, because without the understanding that comes from this learning, we limit the quality, and effect, of our conversations.

Sam was born curious. Over the years, his curiosity has grown beyond measure. The most important thing he's taught me about curiosity, is the need for me to be just as curious about those things and people that I've known for a long time, as I am about something or someone new. Through his example, I've come to appreciate that curiosity is a life-affirming attitude.

Conversations are wonderfully significant because people are wonderfully significant. And questions, managed well, are an integral way of developing insight. They can give us insight into the wonderfully significant person, or people, with whom we are communicating. And they can also give those we are questioning insight into themselves.

The first step in managing questions well, is determining that it is appropriate to ask them. The very least we need is permission. Ideally, our questions are welcomed.

Then we must be clear about the value and purpose of the questions we are going to ask. We need to determine why we are asking every question we do. Are we seeking to learn something for ourselves, or to help someone else learn something? Or both? A useful way to ensure such clarity, is to ask ourselves: for whom am I asking this question – and why? Whatever the purpose, questions are most valuable when formed in the language of those being questioned. To create the best possible chance of this happening they need to be asked using the other person's preferred language patterns and style and be framed within their life experience, not that of the questioner.

Nine useful questions to ask yourself before you begin questioning another are:

- Do I need to ask a question now?
- What am I currently unaware of in this situation?
- What assumptions are driving my behaviour?
- What is the most useful question I can ask now?
- What is the best way to frame and ask the question?
- What size of information do I need to gather?
- What kind of information do I need to gather?
- What kind of state do I wish the other person to enter into by answering my question?
- How does this question help move us closer to the desired end-outcome?

Often, of course, we will need to ask a series of questions. The order in which our questions are sequenced plays an important role in determining the level of focus and engagement of those we are talking with and, consequently, the value of their responses. Appropriate sequencing gives the responder time to warm up to both the task and the topic and helps them to create the most useful emotional state.

Two other factors that influence their willingness to respond and their ability to do so effectively are timing and place. They must feel that there is enough time for this conversation to grow comfortably, and that they are in an appropriate environment for it to do so. In some contexts, our questions might also encourage questions in response. When this happens, we must be willing, and able, to respond to questions as well as ask them.

Here are just some of the different types of question we might use:

Meta questions

These help us to identify a person's underlying frame(s) of reference. They seek insight into what is behind, or what underpins, a person's actions or choices. Questions such as 'What do you believe about...?' and 'What does this mean to you?' are examples of meta questions.

Closed questions

These tend to invite 'yes' or 'no' answers, although they can encourage a little more. For example, 'What is your name?' functions as a closed question. Such questions are often asked to help 'warm up' the respondent at the beginning of an interaction. Although they can be asked at any time, for other reasons.

Open questions

These quite literally 'open the door' for the respondent to provide any answer, with as much detail or explanation as they choose. Open questions tend to require more reflection and thought on the part of the respondent, and can often encourage:

Probing questions

These are questions that 'dig deeper', seeking clarification, explanation, or more detail than has yet been given. Thus, they can provide deeper levels of insight and/or help avoid misunderstandings.

Funnel questions

These are a sequence of questions that begin from a particular point and, according to the purpose of the questioner, either broaden or narrow the focus progressively. For example, the conversation may be narrowed by using closed questions, or widened by using open questions.

No matter what combination you might employ, it's essential that you know when, and how, to stop asking questions. And, when it's your turn to answer questions, ensure you:

- Identify the intention behind the question.
- Use the language of the questioner.
- Ask for clarification if the question is unclear.
- Give answers that are always moving the conversation towards your desired outcome.
- Provide relevant examples to support your answer if appropriate.
- Recognise and defer irrelevant questions.
- Manage closed questions, if necessary, by identifying any underpinning assumption(s) and addressing these.

Finally, whether asking or answering questions, remember that:

Words travel on the breath

I've kept this until last because, for me, it's the most important. You see, whenever we are sharing words, we are always and inevitably sharing breath.
In most Western cultures we tend to breathe out as we speak. In some other cultures words are also spoken on an in-breath. Either way, most of us tend not to notice either our, or the

other person's, breathing patterns because it's too easy to be caught up in what we are saying. Our words and all they represent take precedence over our breathing and all it creates. It's the wrong way round.

Everything that needs to be moved successfully from A to B, from sender to receiver, needs an effective and efficient transport mechanism.

Breath is the transport mechanism for the spoken word. Breath is the constant within the silence, the space from which the best of words grow and through which they travel.

The right words delivered on the wrong breath are unlikely to reach and influence their target, just as a bird caught in a gale is unlikely to fly in a straight line.

In certain situations, we adapt our breath automatically. For example, we instinctively use a forceful exhalation when shouting, a much softer, more gentle exhalation when whispering, and much faster breaths when talking excitedly. We can, though, be far more deliberate and consistent in our use of breath whenever we speak.

We can do this in a number of ways. Firstly, by prioritising our breath over the words, treating our breathing as an integral, vital part of our verbal communication, and choosing and delivering it with the same care we choose our language. This means ensuring that the nature of both our exhalation and inhalation matches the nature of the influence we are seeking to create.

Secondly, when talking with individuals or small groups, we can observe their breathing patterns throughout the interaction. This provides useful insights into how they are feeling.

Then, whenever possible, we can aim to speak when the other person is breathing in, timing our exhalation to their inhalation. This, in turn, fuels the sense that we are breathing our words into the listener(s), rather than just releasing our words without any sense of direction.

So, as we prepare to turn from Principles to Processes, the final headline in this section reads:

Breath is central to interpersonal communication!

That's why breath management is a most powerful way of transitioning from Me to You to Us.

Processes and models

There are eight processes and models I'm going to identify and explain. These are:

- Match – Pace – Lead.
- Deletions, distortions and generalisations.
- The Meta Model.
- The Milton Model.
- An ecology check.
- The Influence Flow: Emotion to Action and Outcomes.
- The OODA Loop.
- TOTE.

Match - Pace - Lead

Here's what these three words mean in this context and how they relate:

Match means to use the other person's preferred communication patterns and, when appropriate and possible, demonstrate how you share and/or understand their perception filters (beliefs, values, aspirations, etc).

Whilst most of us tend not to be consciously aware of our personal communication patterns, we inevitably demonstrate them through the words we use and all aspects of our body language. This allows a person who is skilled at listening and looking to identify and match them. With practice, this can be done very quickly – literally, within minutes. The purpose of matching is to create rapport.

Pace means to listen, question and/or comment in ways that show your interest in, and understanding of, the other person's situation, needs or viewpoint. To understand pacing, think of it quite literally: we are walking in step with the other person. The purpose of pacing is to create trust.

Lead means to take control of the communication flow. The purpose is to direct it towards the most appropriate outcome.

Ultimately, the process of match, pace and lead reminds us that the way in which we deliver our message is at least as important as the message itself.

In the upcoming chapters, I'll identify what to match, how to pace, and when to take the lead.

Deletions, distortions and generalisations

We never tell the whole story. There are two reasons why:

- We never know the whole story in the first place.

In every experience, we give our attention to specific stimuli. We focus on what we decide is most important, or on something that is particularly unusual. They are the factors we remember – although not necessarily with absolute accuracy. Everything else we either delete or generalise. We tell the story from our perspective, often without realising that it is a perspective influenced by our perception filters and our emotional response(s) to the events we are recalling.

- Our audience doesn't need or want to know the whole story.

They don't have the time or the interest. And we don't have the time to tell it, even if we knew it all. Storytellers never give us all the details; they are invariably selective. A novelist or filmmaker does it on purpose; we, on the other hand, delete distort and generalise for the two reasons given above.

In essence, the story of our lives is too complex for us to identify, consider, remember and share every detail. We all need to use a form of linguistic shorthand. So, we delete, distort and generalise.

That's another reason why two people often provide somewhat different accounts of a shared experience.

Great listeners hear these deletions, distortions and generalisations. When it is necessary to do so, they question appropriately, seeking to identify missing details and gain greater insight into the experience and the subconscious communication patterns of the speaker.

The ways we delete, distort and generalise influence us at least as much as they influence those with whom we are talking. They not only reflect our worldview, they continue to reinforce it.

The Meta Model

This is a model that enables us to explore how language influences us, whilst identifying different types of deletions, distortions and generalisations.[27] We can then question to recover missing information and/or create appropriate reframes.

Here's an introduction to the Meta Model, showing some types of deletions, distortions and generalisations with examples of questions you might ask and their purpose:

---

[27] If you want to learn about the Meta Model in more detail, read: Hall, Michael. L. Communication Magic. Exploring the Structure and Meaning of Language. 2002. Crown House Publishing.

Types of Deletion	Examples	Questions	Purpose
Simple deletion (When some information is missing.)	'They don't give me any attention.'	'Who doesn't give you attention?'	Identify who/what has been deleted.
Comparative deletion (When one aspect of a comparison is missing.)	'She's better with technology than me.'	'Better in what ways?' 'Better with what technology?'	As above.
Unspecified verb (A verb that doesn't describe the action.)	'I feel nervous when I present.'	'How do you feel exactly?' 'When do you feel this?'	Identify the details of the verb.
Nominalisation (Turning a verb into a noun.)	'My relationship with my boss is ruined.'	'What aspects of the ways you relate are not working for you currently?'	Return the nominalisation to a process: identify which aspects are not satisfactory.

Types of Distortion	Examples	Questions	Purpose
Mind reading (Claiming to read another's mind.)	'My colleague really has it in for me.'	'How do you know they feel that way?'	Identify specific information / examples.
Complex equivalence (Constructing beliefs out of generalisations; making two experiences equal.)	'She's always quiet around me – she doesn't like me.'	'Why does being quiet signify dislike?' 'Can you think of other reasons why she might be quiet around you?'	Identify how the person equates silence with dislike. Explore other possible reasons for their behaviour.
Cause and effect (Identifying a causal relationship between two, or more, elements.)	'Appraisal meetings with my manager make me nervous.'	'What specifically makes you nervous?' 'Have there ever been moments when you have not been nervous?'	Identify specific causes / origins. Identify counter examples.

Types of Generalisation	Examples	Questions	Purpose
Universal quantifier (A universal generalisation, lacking specific references.)	'That team member never does what I ask them to.'	'Never? Has there ever been a time when they did?'	Identify counter-examples. Explore all aspects of the process.
Modal operator of possibility (A view of what is possible, or not.)	'I could never get a job like that.'	'What prevents you?'	Identify beliefs and causes.
Modal operator of necessity (Words that take away choice.)	'I have to avoid being critical of that member of my team.'	'Always?' 'What would happen if you were critical?'	As above.

By way of a little practice in recognising Meta Model distinctions, read the following speech and identify the:

- Simple deletions.
- Comparative deletions.
- Nominalisations.
- Cause and effect statements.

Here's what the person has to say:

'Whenever I don't succeed, it really bothers me. It always makes me feel like a failure. When I don't reach my goals, I suffer from depression. No wonder I put things off and hesitate about other things. That's why people are better than me and laugh behind my back. I hate being a failure. I ought to just give up; I can't see any future in this.'[28]

The Milton model

This is the opposite of the Meta Model. It is named after, and based on, the work of Milton Erickson, a world-leading hypnotherapist who lived from 1901 to 1980.

Here, the detail and factual precision of the Meta Model are ignored in favour of language that leaves out information and is, therefore, in need of interpretation. The Milton Model focuses on the use of artfully vague language replete with deletions, distortions and generalisations.

Nominalisations, universal quantifiers, modal operators of possibility and metaphor are among the many ways words are used to encourage the listener inwards, so that they actively create meaning from their own experiences.

In short, the Milton Model is the language of trance, which can be understood as an inward focus on a particular stimulus to the exclusion of all else.

You might be surprised to know that you – we – go in and out of trance repeatedly every day of our lives. Have you ever driven to work and wondered how got there?[29] Have you ever found yourself arriving at the car park without any recollection of the specifics of the journey?

I'm guessing that you probably have. And, if so, you spent at

---

[28] The speech is rewritten at the end of this chapter with the examples highlighted.

[29] If you've ever arrived at work and wondered *why* you've gone there, you're asking a very different question. (You might decide to give it some serious consideration, and then read about 'How to get the Job of Your Dreams' in Chapter Four.)

least some of the time driving whilst in a trance. We'd be more likely to call it daydreaming, but that's what daydreaming is: an inward focus to the exclusion of all else.

The deliberate use of the Milton Model to create trance states, is employed perhaps most obviously by hypnotherapists and some other healers and change agents to enable individuals to apply the power of subconscious resources to a specific problem.

Beyond this, the use of deliberately vague language that encourages the listener(s) to create their own meanings, has value in other forms of conversation, ranging from creative business meetings to personal development sessions and business presentations.

Consider this example, imagining that the words are being spoken to you:

'I'm going to ask you a simple and yet very important question. I'm going to give you a minute or two to reflect on your answer and then I'm going to ask for your thoughts.

'Is that OK?

'Good.

'Now, the question is: If you could communicate brilliantly and influence precisely as intended for one hour, with whom would you communicate and what would you aim to achieve? Please understand you can choose any person, or group of people, for any reason. And, before you make your final decision, do realise that you will not only achieve something of great importance, you will also know what it is like to communicate brilliantly and to influence precisely as intended.

'So, please, take the time to reflect on your answer now.

'With whom are you going to communicate? And why?'

The language used throughout that speech is artfully vague. It offers no agreed reference points or context; to engage with it you must go inward to create your own meanings and reasons, and make your own choices.

Whilst doing so you would be revealing to a skilled observer a great deal about your subconscious communication patterns. The observer could then incorporate these into the next part(s) of the conversation to further develop rapport, trust and influence.[30]

An ecology check

John Donne, the 17th century English poet wrote, 'No man is an island.' Several centuries later, Mike Harding, a folk singer and comedian, qualified that by claiming, 'No man is an island apart from Fred Madagascar.'

On reflection, Donne's observation is the more valuable of the two for those of us seeking to communicate and influence positively and powerfully.

We don't exist in isolation. Our words and actions ripple out and influence, often beyond our awareness; often, even, after our death.

We are all part of a range of natural and man-made systems. How we communicate – how we share our presence through space – inevitably impacts those systems. There are always implications, knock-on effects, that need to be identified and evaluated.

That's why it's essential to perform an ecology check every time we create a change in our lives and every time we help others to create a change in theirs.

There's little point creating a positive change in one aspect of your life if it creates a negative effect in another. Equally, there is nothing to be applauded or supported if a person creates positive changes in their life at the expense of negative effects

---

[30] To find out more about the work of Milton Erickson read: Battino, R. & South, T. Ericksonian Approaches. A Comprehensive Manual. 2nd Edition. 2005. Crown House Publishing.

on others.

Ethical communicators understand the need for, and apply, ecology checks. They are essential if your purpose is to create positive outcomes.

The Influence Flow: Emotion to Action and Outcomes

Given that emotional responses are inevitable, we need to know how to create and recognise different individual emotions and, if necessary, create an emotional sequence, or flow, that moves our audience from their current state to the desired state via a series of interlinking emotional shifts.

The elements of an emotional influence flow will, of course, vary according to the other person's starting position, the context and the desired outcome. For example, if we are seeking to establish feelings of Rapport that will lead to Trust and then Commitment, the first state to create might well be Ease.

After all, it's hard, if not impossible, to earn someone's trust if they don't feel at ease with us. Indeed, it's hard to make any positive movement at all if the person is not at ease. And the opposite of ease is dis-ease – when a person is ill at ease. When we think of it like that it doesn't sound very healthy, does it? It doesn't sound very comfortable. And a person is unlikely to feel at ease if they don't feel comfortable.

So, in this example, we need to begin our emotional flow by using the power of words to put someone at their ease. With that as our foundation, we can begin building emotional links in the flow, creating movement towards the desired state from which the person can best take the required action.

Given that, the emotional influence flow might look like this:

Ease...Hope...Interest...Curiosity...Realisation...Trust...
Excitement...Desire...Commitment...

Personally, when creating an emotional influence flow, I find it helpful to categorise the necessary emotions as either primary or secondary.

Primary emotions are the essential drivers of action and change. They are essential if the desired outcome is to be achieved.

Secondary emotions act as the links in the flow that build towards the primary emotions. They are the emotional steps that take the person from one primary emotion to the next. They are necessary because, for example, feeling at ease and feeling trust are two very different things. There is an obvious distance between them. We cover that distance through the creation of secondary, appropriately sequenced emotions.

In the emotional influence flow I offered as an example, Trust and Commitment are the primary emotions.

The person is very unlikely to move on until they trust. This might be trust in me (assuming I'm the person communicating with them), or trust in themselves, or trust in both of us. With trust established, we can then create the links that lead to commitment. This is the absolute willingness to act. It will be fuelled by the feelings of excitement and desire that precede it. These are examples of secondary emotions.

When developing an emotional influence flow, it's also important to understand what emotions can threaten or destroy the secondary or primary emotions involved. Our aim, obviously, is to avoid these. If they do occur, treat the situation as an opportunity to create a magical reframe that transforms the experience into a positive, memorable part of the overall process.

The OODA Loop

This is a great process for turning skilled attention-giving into appropriate action. The OODA Loop combines the following four elements in the following order:

Observation

This is the first step in the OODA loop. You observe both

yourself and the other party. You identify other relevant influences, including environmental factors, availability of resources and timeframes.

Orientation

Once you've gathered sufficient information, put it all into context. Ensure you understand the overall situation; both the big picture and all relevant details.

Decision

Now determine your response; know precisely how it will help you achieve your desired outcomes.

Action

Say and/or do what is necessary; share your message(s) at the time and in the manner best suited to the situation and your desired outcome.

Observe the responses to your actions, orientate, and run through the loop again as many times as are necessary.
If you want to take the lead, go through the OODA Loop faster and more accurately than those with whom you are interacting. As Kipling might have said, 'If you are taking appropriate action when those around are still observing, you are ahead of the game my son.'

TOTE

This stands for:

- **T**est.
- **O**perate.
- **T**est.
- **E**xit.

The TOTE model provides an invaluable framework when creating change, whether that be influencing colleagues, learning something new, or creating and implementing organisational strategy.

The first Test identifies the gap between your current situation and your desired outcome. With that identified, and an ecology check run to ensure the desired outcome is positive on every possible level, Operate to create the necessary change. This operation will, in turn, create feedback.

Test the feedback to see if the desired situation has been achieved fully. If not, Operate again and Test the resultant feedback.

Once it is clear that the desired outcome has been achieved, Exit the strategy.

When you match, pace and lead to create influence, you test, operate and test again until your outcome is reached. Then it's time for the exit stage, right?

And, before we exit from this chapter, we will revisit the speech from earlier, only this time with the:

- Simple deletions identified as (SD).
- Comparative deletions as (CD).
- Nominalisations as (N).
- Cause and effect statements as (C/E).

'Whenever I don't succeed, it (SD) really bothers me. It (SD) always makes me feel like a failure. (N) When I don't reach my goals (SD) I suffer from depression. (N) No wonder I put things off and hesitate about other things. (SD) That's why (C/E) people are better (CD) than me and laugh behind my back. (C/E) I hate being a failure. (N) I ought to just give up; I can't see any future in this.' (SD)

There are other examples of deletions, distortions and generalisations included in those same few lines, which you can identify if you choose. Combined they create what we might think of as a cocktail of toxic ideas and viewpoints, which could:

- Impair and limit the person's performance.
- Create a reinforcing and damaging negative emotional cycle.
- Increase the likelihood of them stopping the activity altogether.

How could we help detoxify the person's current perceptions and change their emotional state and level of performance?

The answer is, through elegant conversations that incorporate any of the appropriate principles, processes, models and skills identified in this chapter and which create a positive emotional flow.

At the heart of this process, of course, are feelings of mutual understanding, respect and closeness – what we often refer to as rapport.

And creating rapport whilst seeking to achieve desired outcomes, is what the next chapter is all about.

Chapter Three

Communicating elegantly

How to create rapport and achieve desired outcomes.

According to the match-pace-lead principle, we match the other person's communication patterns before we pace; we pace before we take the lead.[31]

Here's what to match and how to do it:

Match the other person's communication patterns

If you want to create rapport quickly, match what you hear and what you see.

For all our many similarities, we are wonderfully unique in the ways we express ourselves. Respect that uniqueness by matching what you hear and see.

Treat what follows as a guide. It offers possibilities and examples, not laws or commandments. Use it to remind, and help, you to:

- Avoid being trapped by your own expectations.
- Forget your own perception filters.
- Give skilled attention.
- Look and listen with curiosity and respect.
- Be willing and able to use the preferred communication patterns of others.
- Seek out and respond to feedback.

---

[31] Sometimes you might not need to match before leading. If you are regarded as an authority figure, for example. Or if someone feels they must repay a debt they owe you. Despite this, you might still choose to create likeness and rapport by matching.

- Communicate ethically and elegantly.

And remember: if you want to be a great communicator, attitude and skill are far more important than just knowing a variety of techniques. That's why:

Pattern Recognition is vital.

Only when we have recognised a pattern accurately, can we match it, (to create likeness), or disrupt it, (to create learning and a change in behaviours and outcomes).

Patterns of behaviour are often context dependent. Therefore, we can never assume that we know another human being fully because we accurately identified their preferred communication patterns on one occasion. Tomorrow is another day. The noise within and around them might have changed. The context might be different.

That's why we seek to be comfortable with – even excited by – not-knowing. That's why we communicate best when we are in the moment.

Match with subtlety

Matching should not be obvious to the conscious mind. In other words, the other person shouldn't spot it. If they do, you risk causing offence or amusement. Done well, matching appeals to the other person's subconscious. Everything just seems to fit quite naturally.

Think of an occasion when you met someone for the first time and found yourself relaxed and comfortable almost immediately. Can you say exactly why you got on so well? Probably not. No matter, your subconscious mind recognised the match, and your conscious mind then accepted it.

Generally, we like and feel attracted towards sameness. We learn from difference. Matching creates a feeling of sameness. It makes people want to give you more of their attention.

There are many things we can match. I'm going to begin with

one of the most important. It is:

Matching the other person's voice

This is so important because of:

The power of sound(s).

We are hard-wired from birth, arguably even before, to be influenced by sound. Whilst in the womb, we hear our mother's heartbeat. As new-born infants we are drawn to her voice.[32] It is the first sound of safety.

As we grow, we learn to recognise sounds as key indicators of what is happening in our immediate environment. A raised voice, a siren, the rumble of thunder overhead, a baby's cry, the squeal of car tyres coming to a sudden halt, a partner's sigh of contentment and the first notes of a favourite song, are just a few examples of sounds that draw our attention and change our emotional and physical state.

Sounds are such a powerful influencer they have even been used as a form of torture. In a more nurturing context, great counsellors and therapists, understand that the sound of their voice is at least as significant as the words they use in terms of creating a trusting and safe environment.

Also, as I intimated a moment ago, the sound of a voice is significant in establishing our most meaningful relationships.

I love my wife more than anyone else. I could spend the rest of this book telling you why I think she's so wonderful. Yet, if I hadn't been attracted by her voice, our relationship would never have developed. I would never have come to know and appreciate her many great qualities. Whilst physical attraction plays an essential part in drawing two people together, the sound of each person's voice is also significant.

---

[32] And to her smell, of course.

I made the point earlier that listening was more important than looking. It's true, not just for the reasons I shared in Chapter One, but also because of the primal importance of sound.

There are many ways we can match the voice we are listening to with subtlety and skill. Here are some:

Match the pace and tone

Listen to the different speeds at which people talk. Then practise matching them.

Bear in mind that a person's emotional state will often influence the speed at which they talk, so pace of voice can give us insights into how the other person is feeling. It can also give us insights into how they are experiencing, or remembering, reality.

Listen also to the tone of the person's voice. Hear the times and ways, and recognise when and/or why, their tone changes. Change your tone accordingly.

The approach advocated by Neuro-Linguistic Programming (NLP) suggests that voice pace and tone tend to indicate whether a person is prioritising their visual, auditory or kinaesthetic sense. The indicators are:

Visual: talking very quickly, to keep up with the pictures racing through their mind.

Auditory: using a melodious, rhythmic tone.

Kinaesthetic: talking slowly. Pausing often, to check out how they feel about what they have heard or are about to say.

If, for example, you are matching someone whose tone and pace suggests they are prioritising their kinaesthetic sense, slow down your tempo, pause from time to time, and use language that indicates how you are feeling your way through the conversation.

Again, be guided by the person in front of you. Match them even if their communication patterns are different from anything you have read about or encountered before. Remember, there is no one-size-fits-all approach when it comes to creating elegantly influential conversations.

That's why we sharpen our senses, learn to forget, and approach others with curiosity and respect.

Match the breathing

Breathing is, of course, essential for life. The quality and nature of our breathing also influences the quality and nature of our experience and performance at any given time. Simply put, if our breath isn't appropriate for the task, we usually underperform.

Whilst many of us tend to ignore our breathing, successful communicators focus on it for the two reasons I've already mentioned:

- Words travel on the breath.
- Breath control is integral to creating and maintaining the best state from which to operate.

And also because:

Matching another person's breathing pattern creates a feeling of sameness in a very powerful and subtle way.

It's another example of a primal connection. It's another pattern we can identify and match.[33]

NLP suggests that people prioritising specific senses tend to breathe differently. The indicators are:

Visual: shallow, fast breaths from high in the chest.

Auditory: deeper, rhythmic breathing from the centre of the chest.

---

[33] The skill lies in seeing the person's breathing pattern without making it obvious that you are looking; this requires a mix of visual acuity and the aforementioned subtlety.

Kinaesthetic: slow, deep breathing from the abdomen.

Match phrases and key words

Listen for the most important phrases or words the other person uses and repeat these back when you reply.

If, for example, a person tells you, 'This is the part of my work that I love doing the most,' reply by asking 'What is it about this part that you love so much?' rather than, 'What is it about this aspect that you like so much?'

Match sensory language

NLP suggests that people's words reveal which senses they are favouring. Again, the goal is to identify and match.

Here are some examples of sensory language:

Visual language

- 'I can see what you mean.'
- 'I get the picture.'
- 'I'm looking into the situation.'
- 'Show me how your idea will benefit us.'
- 'Let me shed some light on the matter.'

Auditory language

- 'Your words are music to my ears.'
- 'I hear you loud and clear.'
- 'That rings a bell.'
- 'She's calling the tune.'
- 'We are on the same wavelength.'

Kinaesthetic language

- 'I will be in touch.'
- 'You need to be thick-skinned to work here.'
- 'I have a good feeling about this.'
- 'This project is in danger of falling apart.'

- 'I follow your argument.'

Olfactory and Gustatory language

- 'That left a bitter taste in my mouth.'
- 'I smell a rat.'
- 'You are so sweet.'
- 'That's a hard pill to swallow.'
- 'Something fishy is going on.'

Listen for these and countless other examples. You will hear how people move from one sense to another, and how they use different senses and sequences of senses to discuss different topics.

Avoid labelling individuals as purely 'Visual' or 'Auditory' or 'Kinaesthetic'. We use our senses in various combinations depending on context. For example, if I am choosing a new suit, my buying sequence is: Visual-Visual-Kinaesthetic-Internal dialogue.

It goes like this:

Visual: I like the look of a particular suit.

Visual: I put the suit on and see how I look in it.

Kinaesthetic: I check how the material feels and how I feel wearing the outfit.

Internal dialogue: I tell myself whether I should buy it or not.

Here's a brief story about when I went shopping for a new suit, and the salesman talked me out of it:

I was in a clothes shop in London. A grey pin-striped suit caught my eye. I wanted to see how I would look in it. I wanted to know what it felt like when it was on, and how I felt about myself wearing it. I wanted a little time on my own to consider the pros and cons. I asked a salesman if I could try the suit.

'Certainly sir,' he replied. 'But before you do, just feel the quality of the cloth.'

I put my hand on the sleeve he offered.

'Tell me, sir, isn't the material exquisite?'

I nodded.

'And it's such a good price. We have a special offer today.' He gestured towards a sign in the window.

I nodded again.

'Just ask yourself how much this suit usually retails for, sir.'

I asked myself. It was hard to conjure up a figure; my mind was being swamped with disinterest because my buying strategy had been disrupted.

'Well, I'll tell you,' the salesman said. 'It was £100 more than it is today. What do you think about that, sir?'

'Clearly a goodbye,' I said, walking out of the shop.

As the salesman and I had never met before, I didn't expect him to know my strategy for buying suits. There were, though, alternative approaches to the one he employed. For example, he could have done only what I asked him to, or engaged me in conversation, determined my strategy and then applied it back to me.

Either approach would have kept me in the shop and increased his chances of making a sale. Instead, I walked away from his shop and towards another.

Now let's consider matching things we can see:

Identify and communicate from the other person's *learning side*

The term 'learning side' refers to the side, or angle, from which a person is most welcoming and receptive. Learning sides vary from person to person. Some people are most comfortable if you are on their right, some prefer you to be on their left, and some have no preference and are equally comfortable no matter where you position yourself.

Learning sides develop subconsciously, so for most people they operate as a powerful unconscious habit. If you want to become adept at identifying learning sides, begin with yourself. On reflection, do you prefer to have another person on your right, your left, or doesn't it matter? Consider the layout of your office. Or the position of the armchair you always sit in to watch TV. Or the side of the bed you sleep on. Do you notice a pattern? If you have developed a learning side, you will recognise how it permeates your life.

How can you tell if someone else has a specific learning side? In two ways:

- Observe.
- Test.

If you have the opportunity, simply observe the person in conversation and notice their position relative to the other. Assuming they're wanting to feel comfortable during the interaction, they will have ensured the other person is on their learning side.

If you can't observe – and even if you can and you want to be rigorous in your analysis – test whilst you engage with them.

Talk to the person from different angles and observe their reactions. If their face stays, or becomes, calm, if their shoulders are relaxed, their breathing controlled, if their overall manner and responses are receptive, you are probably on their learning side.

By way of contrast, if you see tension lines appear around their eyes or mouth, if their brow furrows, if their lips appear to 'thin' and their shoulders tense, if their breathing becomes higher in their chest and quickens, you are probably not on their learning side.

If a person has a pronounced learning side, their opposite side will be, well, opposite. If you get on the wrong side of them, their response can be anything from doubtful to dismissive to downright hostile.

A manager at a leisure centre, who had attended a workshop that included learning sides, told me how well it had worked for her. She said:

'I'd spent five minutes trying to persuade my boss to make a particular change. He couldn't have been less interested. Then I realised I'd forgotten to stand on his learning side. As he talked, I changed position and reintroduced my idea. His whole manner changed. He relaxed, smiled, and told me he couldn't agree more. My suggestion was implemented.'

Her experience is a great reminder that, regarding learning sides and, indeed, all aspects of communication, it pays to spot the difference that makes the difference.

Match body language

If we need to create rapport quickly, it's best to match body language deliberately and subtly. Few things can disrupt the rapport-creating process more quickly than crude body language matching.[34] Examples of subtle matching include:

Person A	Person B
Folds their arms.	Crosses one hand over the other.
Crosses their legs.	Crosses their ankles.
Leans forward.	Angles their head forward slightly.
Leans to one side.	Lowers their corresponding shoulder slightly.

With practice, you'll find that matching body language skilfully and elegantly will, like all the other behaviours, become second nature.

Body language can also reflect the senses a person is prioritising. According to NLP the indicators are:

---

[34] By which I mean matching very obviously, rather than making rude gestures.

Visual: hands tend to be held high, gesturing upwards, with eyes often glancing upwards.

Auditory: the head might tip to one side, as if listening. One hand might be held to the side of the face, as if holding a phone.

Kinaesthetic: shoulders are often stooped, as if the weight of the world is upon them.

Mirror body language

Mirroring simply means creating a mirror image of the other person. So, for example, if person A leans slightly to their left, person B might lean slightly to their right. Again, subtlety is essential.

Be congruent when matching sensory language

Aim to combine the language, gestures, eye movements and breathing that match the sensory language you are using. It would, for example, be congruent to use visual language whilst glancing up, talking quickly, taking quick, shallow breaths and gesturing with your hands.

Two significant benefits in recognising and matching sensory language are:

- It helps you to create rapport quickly.
- It enables you to share information clearly.

Disagreements can occur and misunderstandings arise when sensory language is mismatched

Imagine the difficulties that can arise when a person tries to sell an idea using visual then auditory language, to a colleague who favours kinaesthetic and visual sequencing when discussing that particular topic. You might hear something like this:

'David, I want to show you how well the new marketing approach will work. I'm sure, once you get the big picture, you'll be as excited as I am. When I first heard about this, I thought it sounded too good to be true. I assure you though, it is everything I was told it would be.'

'I've already grasped the basic elements of it, Caroline and, to be honest, something just doesn't feel quite right. I need to see it working well before I'm convinced.'

'Just take a look at it one more time. I'll answer any questions you have.'

'My feeling is that right now we need to rein in our enthusiasm for this. At least until I can see how best to use it.'

'But the opportunities are staring us in the face.'

'There are still some significant bridges we have to cross.'

'It's clear that we should go for it. Listen to me!'

'I'm sorry, Caroline. I'm putting my foot down.'

Now, whilst our two fictional characters might never have agreed about the potential value of the new marketing approach, the obvious communication mismatch prevented any meaningful dialogue.

Mirror eye movements

Observe the eye movements the other person makes when they talk about a certain topic, or aspects of that topic. For example, if they look up to their right and then down to their left as they reference certain elements, mirror those eye movements when you mention them.

Now, before identifying a few more things you can match, here's a piece of advice:

Avoid the temptation to put your meanings onto other people's behaviour

When I scratch my head and frown, it usually means I'm concentrating. When Sam scratches his head and frowns it always means he's got an itch.

The point is, the same behaviour done by different people, doesn't always mean they are doing, or feeling or thinking, the same thing. That's why we prioritise pattern recognition, and respect the bespoke nature of communication.

Match areas of agreement and common experiences

Identifying common ground always helps to build rapport.

Match any common values

This is another very powerful rapport-builder.[35]

The more you match another person, the more you come to understand them

Matching, done well, enables you to really understand the other person's perspective – and how they feel when creating and experiencing it. Matching can provide insights into their emotional and physical state(s) and ways of processing, which, in turn, make the transition from Me to You to Us easier to achieve. Sam is, of course, a master at sensing, acknowledging and matching whomever he meets, wherever we are.

'He's right about matching. I don't greet Chris the way I do other dogs. Which I'm sure he appreciates.'

---

[35] Only match values when you can do so ethically.

Next we pace:

The better you match, the quicker you pace, the sooner you lead

Pacing links matching and leading. Pace only for as long as you need to. Aim to make it as brief as possible. Then use your influence to lead.

Create more-the-more patterns of agreement when you pace

A more-the-more pattern is simply a repetitive process or activity. These patterns can be positive or negative. We tend to refer to them as either virtuous or vicious circles. Exercising regularly is an example of a more-the-more pattern. So is smoking cigarettes.

More-the-more patterns occur in communication, too. One of the most useful to create when seeking to influence someone, is a more-the-more pattern of agreement. This is achieved by encouraging the other person to say 'Yes', or show agreement, repeatedly.

Think for a moment of the workplace.

Wouldn't you say that one of the key roles of management is to establish positive more-the-more patterns throughout the organisation?

Isn't it likely that the more positive more-the-more patterns an organisation creates, the more effectively and efficiently it will run?

Isn't that, in a broad sense, the aim of all organisations?

Have you just answered 'Yes' to those questions?

And if you answered 'Yes' to that last question, you've now agreed four times in a row, haven't you? [36]

----

[36] And that makes five...

So, if you want to develop rapport in any context, explore ways of creating genuine more-the-more patterns of agreement.

Think of how many different ways people can say, or show, that they agree with you. Be sure that the agreements you elicit arc congruent.

Sometimes people might agree because they are afraid to say otherwise. Sometimes people agree even though they are uncomfortable doing so. Sometimes they don't even mean it. Recognise and identify the differences.

A more-the-more pattern of agreement is, at best, only one indication of rapport. Yet, if you have matched elegantly and subtly, and paced the other person into a more-the-more pattern in which you are in frequent agreement, they are more likely to give you permission to take the lead.

When they do:

Know your destination

I worked with a manager once who was always trying to create new initiatives, to lead his staff in new directions. Unfortunately, he was never certain in his own mind about which precise direction to go in, for how long and why. He lacked clearly defined, positive outcomes that supported and reflected the organisation's overall strategy. The result was that he led his staff into circles of confusion and, eventually, anger.

He told me, 'My staff are right behind me.'

And they were. A long, long way behind. He stormed off, directionless, expecting others to follow. His team hung back, telling him silently where to go.

When you lead, ensure you are taking others with you

Leading simply means creating the desired level of influence on the appropriate people. We can provide leadership in any context.

To increase your chances of leading successfully, give skilled attention, match, pace and create positive more-the-more patterns. When you lead, keep the people you need by your side. You might achieve this by:

- Sharing information, responsibility and/or ideas.
- Demonstrating authority appropriately.
- Asking and/or answering questions.
- Creating positive states.
- Creating positive more-the-more patterns.
- Continually matching and pacing.
- Recognising, respecting and responding to individual or group concerns or needs.
- Emphasising benefits.

Take the lead one step at a time

People give you permission to take the lead. You need to earn and then maintain their trust if they are to extend that permission, so influence at an appropriate pace, using the most appropriate communication styles.

The phrase 'one step at a time' does not imply slowness. Sprinters and turtles both go one step at a time. Aim to move as fast as the situation allows, whilst keeping your significant others with you.

When you are leading, sequence information appropriately

Different people prefer to receive information sequenced in different ways. Whilst we may not be consciously aware of our preference, we do recognise quickly when we find information difficult to grasp.

One way we can understand, and then manage, this is by dividing information into the following categories:

- Concept.
- Structure.

- Use.

Some people prefer to be given information in that order. I'm one of them. If you want me to be interested in something new, tell me about the conceptual framework first, and then describe the structure, attributes and content. Finally, show me how to use it. That does it for me every time. Other people prefer to go structure, use, and concept. Or use, concept, structure.

If you want to lead people into accepting new information, or systems or structures, discover first how they prefer their information to be sequenced. Then meet that need.

If you are leading a team, vary your information sequencing to ensure everyone understands the key elements

When talking to a team, vary your sequencing of concept, structure and use. And repeat the key points using different language styles. (For example, visual, auditory and kinaesthetic.)

Engage in both dialogue and discussion

The two words have very different meanings.

Dialogue stems from the Greek *Dialogos*. *Die* meaning 'through' and *logos* meaning 'the word', or 'the meaning'. When people engage in dialogue, they put their assumptions to one side and search together for meanings and insights they may not be able to access individually. In dialogue, people tend to regard each other as colleagues; sometimes they will employ a facilitator to help maintain the context and focus.

Discussion, on the other hand, stems from the Medieval Latin *discussionem*, meaning 'examination'. To get a sense of discussion imagine a verbal table tennis game in which one person, or group, is seeking to prove their point and win the conversational game.

Managers seeking to encourage creativity and change within their teams need to create the appropriate combination of dialogue and discussion. There are times when dialogue will be more productive than discussion, and vice versa. The manager's task is to recognise which is required and how to stimulate and control it.

Whether engaged in discussion or dialogue, there are some words that need to be handled with care, and some that it makes sense to use frequently. Here are a few examples:

A word to handle with care: *But*

But is used in discussion. When someone either begins a sentence with the word *but*, or introduces it halfway through, they usually go on to disagree with what the other person has said. And we often sense the word *but* approaching; like a wave rolling into shore, it's hard to disguise.

Essentially, *but* is used to score points rather than facilitate a sharing of ideas and meaning. So, when you want dialogue rather than discussion, banish the word 'but' from the conversation.

A word to handle with care: *Try*

Try is the present tense of a past failure.[37] When you talk or think in terms of what you will *try* to do, you begin laying the groundwork for potential failure.

'But it's only a word!' I hear some of you say. (Well, obviously I can't actually hear you saying it. I'm just imagining the table tennis ball whizzing in my direction.) 'Single words don't have that much power!'

Really?

When I asked my wife if she would marry me, she replied with

---

[37] Unless you're playing rugby.

a single word. It was the greatest sound I'd ever heard, and it created the greatest feeling I'd ever felt.

When my friend was given the result of a series of medical tests he'd undergone, he heard only a single word. I know, in that moment, he was devastated. Sometime later, when he asked his consultant if he was in remission, the one-word answer made him cry with joy.

Now, I accept that we tend to use words in multiples. Yet there are many occasions when the power of an individual word stands out. I also accept that inappropriate words delivered in an inappropriate manner by a person with whom we are not in rapport, or who doesn't have any power over us, might not be too influential. (Depending, of course, on how we are feeling at the time and the context within which it happens.)

However, inappropriate words delivered by a person to whom we have given power, or with whom we share rapport, can have a pronounced effect.

Let me tell you a story about the word *try* and its effect when employed within a carefully sequenced communication:

I had taught a martial arts class in which I had mentioned how words can affect minds and bodies, and therefore influence performance. One of the students, an experienced male black belt named John, was sceptical and dismissive.

So, we did a quick demonstration.

I asked him to identify his favourite technique. It was a front hand punch. I told him I would discuss it with him in what would appear to be a positive and motivational way. If he noticed me say, or do, anything that was in any way counterproductive, he had to point it out. I promised that by the end of the conversation he would be incapable of doing the punch to his usual standard.

John agreed to the test.

We talked for several minutes. He was happy throughout that I was being positive and helpful. When came to demonstrate the punch, his technique was only half as good as usual. When he tried again, it was worse still. He couldn't understand why. I'll tell you some of the reasons.

Firstly, we had rapport. Secondly, Steve regarded me as an accomplished teacher and, therefore, as an authority figure. Thirdly, I exhibited absolute certainty about the result of our test; I promised him that his punch would deteriorate. Given the previous two points, he found that impossible to ignore. Fourthly, I chose my words with great care. Amongst other things, I said that I wanted him to '*try* really hard' to do a good punch.

Now, as I've already mentioned, *try* is easily associated with failure. To *try* hard was the opposite of what Steve needed to do physically. His body needed to be relaxed, not hard, when he punched.

The word 'to' also sounds the same as the word 'two'. So, on one level, the instruction '*try* hard to' means 'get twice as tense as necessary and fail.'

Please understand, my use of the word *try* was only one part of the complete process. However, it was an important part.

A word to handle with care: *Don't*

Whatever you do, *don't* think of the name of my dog now. And when you do, *don't* remember what breed he is.[38]

The basic rule here is, well, pretty basic: only tell people what you want them to do. If I say to you, '*Don't* think of a green horse, think only of a red one,' the instruction 'think of a green horse' overpowers the first word '*Don't*.' Your mind creates, and then has to dismiss, the image of a green horse before it can create a red one.

In most situations it is inappropriate to speak in ways that

---

[38] I'm guessing you just remembered that his name is Sam, and that he's a Staffordshire Bull Terrier.

make people think of what not to do. It's far more productive to direct people only towards the most desired thought, behaviour or outcome.

Here's an example of when the word *don't* created several undesired outcomes:

During a visit to my GP, I found myself waiting nervously whilst he compiled the results of several tests and checked through a couple of books. He frowned and scratched his head. I remembered Sam and hoped he was concentrating, rather than itching.

Finally, he said, 'Well, Mr Parker...' (Which, to be honest, was precisely the result I wanted to hear. Unfortunately, he hadn't finished.) '...Well, Mr Parker you *don't* have to worry about this being epilepsy.'

Epilepsy!

It hadn't crossed my mind that I might have epilepsy. Until then. Suddenly the single word 'epilepsy' was thundering across my mental landscape with the fury of a green horse that wasn't going to get out of the way.

Even though I was cognitively aware of his inappropriate use of the word *don't* and the implications – telling someone 'You *don't* have to worry', is precisely the same as telling them '*Don't* think of a green horse', you are actually encouraging them to do the thing you want them to avoid – it didn't help me; my emotions had already been released by his word-spell.

Epilepsy!

My heartbeat quickened. My mouth dried. I began to sweat. (Very discreetly.) I didn't hear the next couple of things he said, because I was too busy worrying about epilepsy.

By the end of our session, I had recovered my senses enough to realise that a) I wasn't suffering from a serious illness and b) my GP needed a quick lesson about the power of communication.

We had a chat. I referred to some appropriate scientific research about the wonderful significance of conversations.

116

We talked about how communication influences emotional states. I recommended a couple of books. When I left his office, he was looking as thoughtful as when I arrived, but for a very different reason.

Now let's move on to some words that are good to use:

A word to use: *And*

And is the opposite of *but*. *And* acknowledges and builds off at least some aspect of what has just been said. In doing so, it helps to create dialogue.

A useful practice if you want to experience the impact *and* has on subsequent words, is to make a commitment to avoid saying the word *but* for a day and to replace it with the word *and*. You might be surprised by the changes that forces you to make.

A word to use: *Do*

Do provides positive and clear direction. When you tell someone what it is they need to *do*, especially when using their preferred communication patterns, you create focus and understanding.

The request, '*Do* think of a green horse', goes straight to the point and significantly limits the chance of any misunderstanding. As a general rule, *do* tell people precisely what you need them to *do*, what you need them to think about and/or what the desired outcome is.

If combined with other appropriate words, appropriately sequenced and delivered through the most appropriate communication channels, the word *do* can really help to spare you the costs of miscommunication.

A word to use: *Just*

Just implies that something is easy, that it is accessible and achievable.

One Saturday night, before my stepdaughter went into town to meet her friends, she said to me, 'Could you *just* give me an extra £20, so that I'm sure to have enough money for a taxi for the journey home? Oh, by the way, I've tidied up your study...'

Her use of the word *just* was intended to make her request seem simple and small. She supported it with two other influencers. The first was connecting the extra money to the need for her safety. Secondly, she added in the principle of Reciprocity. She had done something for me, so I felt as if I owed her.

The combination led to the outcome she expected. I decided that £20 probably wasn't quite enough and gave her £30 instead.

A word to use: *Because*

Because has power because we are conditioned to expect reasons to follow in its wake.

Because is a justifying word, it explains and persuades. Research suggests that, when we ask someone to do us a favour, we are more likely to get agreement if we offer a reason or two in support of our request. Reasons tend to be preceded by the word *because*. Consequently, we tend to automatically associate *because* with justification and, therefore, we are subconsciously conditioned towards acceptance whenever we hear the word.

Because is a powerful word to use; we *just* know it is instinctively – *and* the research tell us so.

A word to use: *Now*

Now summons immediacy in the way that no other word does. Used and sequenced well it draws the listener into the moment and can compel action. It can transform what might otherwise be interpreted as a suggestion into an instruction.

Delivered with brilliant timing – which is when the listener is fully receptive and motivated – *now* can spark a positive explosion of activity.

A word to use: *Yes*

Yes can be used to agree or disagree. Sometimes, for example, we can use *yes* to confirm silently to ourselves or publicly to others that we have a different viewpoint and are refusing to engage in a certain idea or activity.

In contrast, *yes* can also signal a shared understanding or commitment. *Yes* can let people know they have been heard or understood; it can instil confidence, hope or relief. In dialogue, *yes* can be combined with another word to create one of the most powerful phrases we can think or say. That phrase is:

'Yes and...'

It's a phrase that, perhaps above all others, marks the attitude of a great communicator. I say this because *Yes and*:

- Acknowledges what is happening or has just been said.
- Reflects a commitment to build off what has been said, or what has just happened.
- Underpins the desire to learn from feedback.

This requires the ability to give skilled attention, to know how to remove the blinkers of our perception filters and be fully present in the moment.

A *Yes and* attitude is essential if we are going to apply the OODA Loop and TOTE swiftly and accurately. It reflects a willingness to adapt as and when the situation requires it. It encourages curiosity. It's another practice that helps us to transition from the division of Me and You to the connectivity of Us.

Manage embedded commands and embedded questions.

Embedded commands are presuppositions and instructions camouflaged as statements. A presupposition is a form of belief or assumption. Presuppositions tend to be heard in sentences containing the words 'if', 'when' and 'since'. If you want to challenge a presupposition simply reveal it for the belief it is, and ask how, or why, it has come to be accepted as a fact by the other person.

The power of embedded commands stems from the way they can influence the physical and emotional state of the listener, their perception of the context, and their subsequent behaviour.

Sometimes people deliver an embedded command without realising that's what they are doing. These commands can be either positive or negative.

Listen to the phrase: 'You won't find this too difficult'.

It contains the presupposition that there will be a degree of difficulty involved. Yet it's entirely possible that the speaker's intention was to reassure the listener that the task would be easy. If spoken by a respected authority figure and/or someone with whom the listener has rapport, this embedded command might well be difficult to ignore.

If our fictitious friend Caroline says to David, 'I don't know when you will think about this again, but whenever it is I'm sure you'll find that you have a good grasp of the situation,' she is embedding commands. They are:

- 'You will think about this again.'
- 'It will make sense when you do.'

The phrase 'make sense' can, like many others, be delivered on its own as either an embedded command or as an embedded question. The intonation of our voice determines which it is.

Let's take a simple example to demonstrate this. Imagine that you have just shared some information with a colleague, or explained to a child why they should behave in a certain way. You finish by saying, 'Make sense.'

If, when you say those words, you lower your intonation it

becomes a command. You are subliminally telling the other person to work it out in their own mind and recognise the value; you are presupposing that they can, and will, do this.

If your intonation goes up as you say the words it becomes a question, and the other person will almost certainly recognise it as such. At that point you are asking them for their opinion, you are encouraging the possibility of discussion or dialogue.

When Caroline continues, 'Although David, I wonder if you already have a sense about which of the two options you will choose?' She is now embedding a question, along with the presupposition that one of the options will be chosen.

To manage embedded commands and questions well, we can:

- Recognise them and challenge the associated presupposition(s) if they are deemed unhelpful.
- Apply them to encourage and enable positive change in others.

Practise safely

In other words, develop your ability in situations that are of relatively limited importance. Only apply your skills within the workplace or with your family, when you have developed an appropriate level of proficiency. To do otherwise, is to risk making errors that could have significant consequences.

So, no matter how enthusiastic you are about developing your communication skills, please be disciplined and deliberate in your approach.

As with all types of training and practice, there is a balance to be achieved between quality and quantity. Personally, I would recommend the 'little and often' approach. Achieving, and maintaining, high levels of sensory acuity can be fatiguing, especially when we are not used to doing so, and, inevitably, the quality of our performance and learning diminish as our energy levels drop. It's better, then, to practise briefly and selectively.

We interact with many people throughout the day so there are countless opportunities to choose from. I recommend that you select a specific attribute or skill and work on it until you feel you've made sufficient progress.

You might, for example, decide to determine the learning side of your local shopkeeper, a barman, or a market researcher who stops you in the street.

When you can do this, select another attribute or skill and develop it. Over time you will find yourself combining your abilities and associated techniques instinctively.

The information you need to develop your face-to-face communication skills is all around you.

Just go for it.

'If you don't think small things can make a big difference, you've never had fleas.'

Chapter Four

Influential Conversations

Managing the building blocks of influence.

Having talked about the importance of conversations, it's time now to address these building blocks in detail. We'll begin by dividing conversations into the following types:

- Informal and unplanned (eg a chat in a corridor).
- Informal and planned (eg a chat over lunch).
- Formal and planned (eg interviews and meetings).
- Visual and non-visual (eg face-to-face or on the phone).
- Dependent on technology (eg a video call).

They are all of equal importance because, in the grand scheme of things, our different types of conversation combine to create the outcomes we achieve. They also combine to create the person we have, and will, become.

Let's just take a moment to remind ourselves that we are all the result of the myriad conversations we've had throughout our lifetime: conversations with family members, friends, colleagues, authority figures, teachers, mentors and, even, strangers. And we, in turn, have played our part in shaping others through our conversations with them.

Conversations are like stones being thrown into water; they create the ripple effect I mentioned at the very beginning. We need to direct and measure their flow if we are to influence as desired. A single conversation can spark many others and be the force behind a tidal wave of change.

Irrespective of which type of conversation you are preparing for, or are engaged in, the same two questions need to be asked and answered:

- How do I want the other person to feel when this conversation is over?

- What do I want them to say or do because of this conversation?

These questions remind us that:

- We need to have clearly defined outcomes.
- All communication creates emotional responses first.
- Conversations never exist in a vacuum.

Audience analysis, ahead of time if possible, and always throughout the conversation, is essential for both recognising and managing the emotional state of others.

Also, understanding how an individual conversation fits into a greater context enables us to determine our immediate goals and recognise when and how to end the interaction.

We'll talk more about the importance of great endings when we explore business presentations. For now, suffice to say it's important that we end conversations at the right time in the right way. Endings really, really matter. Shakespeare told us that and he certainly knew a thing or two about the power of words. In Richard II, he wrote, 'More are men's ends mark'd than their lives before'. He also observed, 'The last Malteser in the bag tastes the best.'[39] And I don't think you can argue with either.

Anyway, let's transition from the Bard to business. Here are some ways you can communicate successfully when engaged in:

- Interviews.
- Meetings.
- Conflict resolution.

---

[39] Shakespeare actually wrote, 'As the last taste of sweets, is sweetest last.' I just happen to like Maltesers.

And when:

- Delegating.
- Talking on the phone.
- On a video call.
- Delivering customer service.
- Leading others.

By way of an additional pre-introduction to these topics, it's vitally important that I emphasise this simple truth: you can take everything that follows, adapting slightly as necessary, and apply it to every aspect of your life.

And I mean, every aspect. Where's the life-value in using the power of conversations brilliantly in the workplace and yet failing to do so at home, or with your friends, or, even, to help total strangers?

Interviews

Interviews can make those involved uncomfortable and tense. So, whether you are the interviewer or interviewee, you need to create the most useful state within yourself and remember that interviews, like most forms of communication, usually start before they start and end after they have ended.

What follows focuses on recruitment interviews and considers them from the perspectives of both applicant and employer. However, the processes, principles and tips can also be applied, sometimes with just a little adjustment, to all other types of interview.

When you are the applicant:

It's important to remember two things:

- Match-Pace-Lead is the winning process when applying for a new job.
- It's essential to make a great first impression at every stage of the recruitment and selection process.

These are two of the three reasons why I regard applying for a new job, even the written elements, as a form of extended conversation.

The third reason is that whenever we apply for a new position, we are seeking to influence certain individuals to come to the decision we need them to. Also, by approaching it this way, we avoid the trap of thinking that we are applying to an organisation.

Whenever we do that, we tend to forget that every organisation is just a collection of human beings, all of whom can be influenced by conversation and communication. To make matters worse, we can even let ourselves be intimidated by the impression the organisation creates. Sometimes we can be intimidated to such an extent that we don't even apply for the job in the first place!

Better, then, to remember that:

People buy from people[40]

and to treat our application as a series of conversations through which we will influence elegantly and as intended.

Find the right job by knowing the life you want to live, and by identifying your hierarchy of criteria

Preparation for a recruitment interview involves two types of audience analysis:

- Self-analysis, considering firstly if the job is right for you and, if so, identifying your strengths and weaknesses in the light of the Person Specification.
- Researching and analysing the organisation, key

---

[40] I'm using the word *buy* here in its broadest sense, to mean the acceptance of ideas, rules, plans, possibilities etc, rather than simply the purchasing of an object or a service.

individuals and, if possible, the interviewers.

How do you know if the job is right for you? By taking a step back and asking yourself the question:

'What is the life I most value and need?'

If you are wondering what this has to do with conversations, let me explain.

At the beginning of our time together, when talking about the importance of our communication, I wrote that communication shapes the present and creates the future.

Our career path is an integral part of both. In order to be our own careers guide, we need to give ourself some skilled attention. We need to ask the right questions, identify and manage any limiting perception filters and presuppositions, and know how to apply an ecology check.

In short, our intrapersonal communication influences the dreams we have and the decisions we make. I believe we owe it to ourselves, and our loved ones, to get it right.

That's why, whenever I work with a client to help them identify and then get a new job, I begin by asking them how they want their life to be in 2, 3, 5 or, even, 10-years' time.

We talk about this in detail. I ask for a clear, detailed vision of their most desired future. I insist that, every time they say, or think, the phrase 'My career', or 'My job' or anything similar, they immediately follow it with the thought, 'My life'. Because that is what we are planning: a person's life.

And, whilst our career is a significant part of our life experience, it certainly isn't the only one – and, if push came to shove, I suspect that for most of us it wouldn't be the most important.

Too often, societies create communication norms that define success as being based solely on the professional accomplishments of the individual. Too often, the communication we encounter encourages us to create a false split between our professional and personal self. And the power of social proof adds its weight to this pressure.

Consequently, we find ourselves talking about our work life and our personal life. We persuade ourselves that the two are separate; that somehow the inevitability of influence does not apply. We can even go so far as to believe that it's acceptable for our personal life to suffer so that we can be successful at work.

Such duality is at best cumbersome and at worst, dangerous. The Me-You-Us approach emphasises connectivity and connection. The different aspects of my life experience are inter-related; they influence each other; they change, combine and create the person I believe myself to be, they affect how I perform, how I am perceived, and how I influence others. Understanding this is an integral part of understanding the Me aspect of Me-You-Us.

I do accept that our professional role influences our sense of identity. And I also accept that there might be times when one aspect of our life demands more of our attention and energy than others. The challenge lies in how to best manage the totality of our professional and personal life experience.

That's why, when my client has created their vision for the future, I ask them to carry out an ecology check. I would urge you to do the same. Once you have done that, and you are happy and motivated by the results, it's time to ask yourself a more specific question:

'What are the things I most want from my work?'

Create a list. Then prioritise it. This list is your hierarchy of criteria. Once it is established, look for jobs that match your list as closely as possible. Here's how you go about that process: Ask yourself, 'What do I want from a job?' and make a note of your answers. (These are your criteria.).

You identify your criteria by asking, for example, 'Do I want a job that:

- Only requires me to use my current skills (or some of them)?
- Is office-based?
- Gives me a leadership role?
- Provides on-going training?
- Requires creativity and new ways of doing things?
- Enables me to work alone primarily?
- Requires me to be a team member?
- Is mainly repetitive?
- Guarantees regular feedback?
- Provides a certain level of income? (Specifically how much?)
- Has a clear structure and opportunity for progression?
- Is based in a certain country, or in a certain part of a country?'

Once you have established your criteria, turn your notes into a prioritised list.

Do this by asking yourself:

'If I can only have 'this' (criteria no1) or 'this' (criteria no2) which would I choose?'

Imagine keeping hold of the criteria you select and then ask yourself the same question again about it and criteria no3.
Again, keep hold of the criteria selected and challenge it against the next criteria on your list.
Do this until you have questioned the criteria you are holding against all the others. This is then your most important criteria. Write it down as no1 on your prioritised list.
Repeat the process with the remaining criteria until your prioritised list is complete.
Then leave your hierarchy of criteria list alone for a week or two.
After that time, read it again and notice your emotional

response(s). Does it still feel right? If so, base your job-hunting on it. If not, repeat the list-creating process until it does.

Then, search for jobs that match your criteria – especially the ones at the top of your list.

Once you find the job of your dreams, it's time to:

Play the Getting a Job game!

When you find a job that you want to apply for, there are four things you need to remember:

The first thing

The first and most important point is that getting a job is like playing a game. It's a competition. And, like every competition, people who know how to play, who have the relevant skills, who know the rules and who know how to adapt, win more often than those who don't. There are effective, efficient and very productive ways to play the game. And then there's just potluck. By knowing how to play the game well, we minimise the luck factor.

The second thing

Having the required qualifications and the relevant experiences and skills serves only one purpose in the Getting a Job game: they allow you to play.

Nothing more. Nothing less. It doesn't mean that you will be good at the game. It is certainly no guarantee of success. The probability is that if you meet the role requirements so will many others. Which leads us on to:

The third thing

Unlike other games, there is no limit as to how many people can play the Getting a Job game at one time. Sometimes only a handful of individuals will apply for a job. Sometimes it will be hundreds. Either way, the third thing is simply this: there is only ever one winner. There are no runners-up medals, no podium places for losers. The good news, however, is:

The fourth thing

The ideal candidate doesn't exist.

Advertisements, job descriptions and person specifications reflect an organisation's dream candidate; the person who has everything they need. This is a fictional character.[41]

You don't have to meet all the role requirements perfectly to get the job. You just need enough of what they are looking for, and then play the game better than your competition.

So, the question is, how will you know when to enter the game and when to sit back?

Determine this by studying the essential and desired experiences and skills identified in the Person Specification. If you have a sufficient number, supported by a range of the desired qualities, then apply.

If you're wondering what number is sufficient, truth to tell there isn't a single right answer. Personally, when working with individuals to help them progress their career, if the person has more than 60% of both the essential and desired qualities, I always feel that we're good to join the game.

At which point it's time to produce a CV and some form of letter of application.

Writing a CV

Matching the employer's needs is central to getting the job of your dreams.

This means matching far more than just the role requirements. It also means matching their values, their priorities and their

---

[41] Unless they are describing a colleague in situ who is also applying for the job.

language patterns. It means, if possible, identifying their motivational and decision-making tendencies and matching these, too.[42]

All of this, of course, requires you to do a thorough analysis of the organisation and the individuals who will be making, or influencing, the final decisions. And social media makes it easy to do! We can learn lots about the attitudes, values and experiences of the individuals we need to impress by finding and studying their various social media communications.

The matching process starts with your CV.

A useful presumption is that the reader glances, scans and only then reads your CV in detail. So, if you want to ensure they continue reading, impress on the first glance.

Researchers suggest that, when it comes to recruitment interviews, we create first impressions that stick – both positively and negatively – in anything from ten seconds to five minutes.

Your CV will make a first impression, too.

Given that, create, design and produce your CV with the same attention to detail that an advertising expert does a magazine ad or a billboard. Work on the premise that you have only a second or two to grab the viewer's attention and then turn it swiftly into interest.

That means how your CV looks is really important. If the font size is too small, if it lacks relevant and clear sub-headings, if there are spelling errors, you run the risk of being dismissed because of your first impression.

Every element of your CV, both in terms of presentation, structure and content, must be justifiable. Consider every word, phrase, sentence, sub-heading, example and bullet-point

_____

[42] Examples of decision-making and motivational tendencies are shared in Chapter Five.

and ask yourself:

- What purpose does this serve?
- What message is this sharing?
- How does this demonstrate ways in which I match the role and/or the organisation?

Ensure you:

- Avoid jargon and acronyms.
- Only list relevant dates, facts and qualifications.
- Use positive, relevant words such as 'Marketed', 'Led', 'Developed', 'Collaborated', 'Networked', 'Created', 'Initiated'.
- Avoid phrases that imply a lack of commitment, enthusiasm or success, such as: 'Worked in', 'Duties', 'tried'.
- Use sub-headings and vocabulary that are achievement driven; highlight your Responsibilities and Achievements.
- Use the organisation's language wherever possible.
- Use bullet-point lists and brief, connecting paragraphs if necessary.

Ensure also that your content includes your:

- Name, address and contact details.
- Personal profile.
- Relevant education.
- Relevant accomplishments and experience.
- Relevant activities and interests.
- Skill summary. (Key words only.)
- Referees. (Choose individuals whose title, role and/or experience are most likely to influence the employer positively.)

When creating a CV that matches, or exceeds, the requirements and expectations of the organisation:

- Match explicitly the requirements of the Person Specification and Job Description.
- Demonstrate how your experience and skill set meets the 'Essential' criteria first and then the 'Desired' criteria. (Address the criteria in the order they are listed by the organisation.)
- Give a specific example (or two) to support every claim you make regarding your experience and skills.

Once your CV is done, it's time to write your supporting document.

Writing a letter of application

The purpose of this is to:

- Reinforce and develop the points and messages you shared in your CV.
- Highlight your understanding of the organisation's needs and priorities.
- Address their requirements in the order they identified them.
- Provide examples that 'prove' the assertions you make.

Write this document using the language of the organisation, incorporating their key phrases. Then edit it thoroughly.

Finally, ensure you get your application in before the deadline; few employers are tolerant of lateness.

Managing the recruitment interview

Remember throughout that, for all the pre-determined structure, level of formality, requirements and rules, a recruitment interview is just a type of conversation.

When we are being interviewed, we are talking with other

people. We will influence, one way or another. And we, in turn, will be influenced. Our goal is to manage both to the best of our ability.

We do this most successfully by being in the moment, focusing on the process, and remembering that ethical communication is a form of:

Well packaged honesty.

This is at least as important when we are seeking to win the Getting a Job game, as it is in every other communication context.

The principle of well packaged honesty is based on the important understanding that the truth alone is no guarantee of success. The truth must be structured, sequenced and delivered well for it to be influential.

If we want to come first in the Getting a Job game, we need to share meaningful messages, supported by truthful examples that highlight both our skills and our experiences. We need to do this consistently throughout the process – remembering, of course, that this process, just like all others, starts before it starts.

Before the interview

To prepare for the big day, revisit your research about the organisation; remind yourself about their mission, culture, values, language preferences, strategies and key individuals. Remind yourself, too, of the power of first impressions.

Then review the Job Description and Person Specification; be clear about the skills and attitudes you need to demonstrate and discuss.

Finally, review your CV and letter of application; remind yourself of the key points you have made; consider how you will develop/'prove' these if required.

Use the above to:

- Identify the most likely questions and prepare your answers.
- Prepare a question (or two) of your own.

Then:

- Practise with a trusted friend.
- Plan your journey to the organisation, adding in additional time in case of delays.
- Prepare everything you need, documents, clothing, petrol in your car, travel tickets etc, the day before.
- If an informal visit is offered before the interview day, take it. And be as well prepared for this as if it were the real thing – because it is.

Work on the premise that:

- The shortlisted applicants are not equal in the eyes of the employer.
- Some individuals will have impressed more with their CV and written application than others.
- Someone will be in pole position; someone will be at the back of the grid.
- All of that can change on the day.
- The elegant delivery of well packaged honesty is very hard to beat.

On the day of the interview

Remind yourself once again that every communication starts before it starts and ends after it ends. So:

- If travelling to the venue on public transport, be aware of the possibility that you might be sitting next to, or near, employees of the organisation you are visiting. Behave, therefore, as if you are under scrutiny.
- Arrive early and keep out of the way.

- Present yourself as required at the time stated.
- Be alert throughout – for example, whilst waiting in reception, if taken on a tour of the facilities, and during lunch. Operate on the principle you are being studied and assessed at all times.
- Maintain this state until you have left their premises (and beyond if travelling on public transport).

When being interviewed:

- Demonstrate a relaxed, confident manner.
- If you are wanting to use postcard notes as prompts, ask for permission first.
- Use the questioner's key words/phrases in your answer(s).
- Always give supporting examples to 'prove' your assertions.
- Determine when it is necessary to provide big picture answers and when to talk in detail.
- Ask for clarification if questions are unclear.
- If there is an interview panel, ensure you engage all members during every answer. (Begin and end by addressing the questioner.)
- Ensure, too, that you appeal to a variety of decision-making tendencies.
- Take every opportunity to highlight your understanding of the organisation and the role requirements - and to show how you match their needs and values.
- Ensure your question shares a final positive message about yourself.
- Maintain your attention and focus when, and after, the interviewer signals closure.

Remember:

An employer's obligation is to find and employ the person who is clearly the best fit for their business. This person needs to match their corporate culture, their organisation beliefs and values, as well as having (enough of) the required skills and experiences.

So, as with your CV, only share information that is relevant to the employer; make it easy for them to offer you the job.

And when they do, trust your gut instinct. Only accept the post if it feels right. You are allowed to say, 'No' based on your experience during the day.

The Getting a Job game is always a game of two hands.

On the one hand, applicants are keen to win the job of their dreams. (Assuming they have identified and evaluated their hierarchy of criteria accurately.) On the other hand, employers are keen to attract and engage the most suitable individual. The game concludes best when both hands come together in mutual agreement and delight.

So, if you find yourself doubting the suitability of the role and/or the organisation, exercise your right to raise your hand, metaphorically speaking, and request a time-out to reflect. And if you decide that it isn't the dream job you believed it to be, wave goodbye.

After the interview

Assess your performance twice: firstly, from an immediate, emotional perspective and, a few days later, in a rational, clinical manner. Notice any differences between the two and consider reasons for these.

Beyond your own assessment, expect – request if necessary – feedback from the organisation. Compare it with your self-evaluation.

Playing the Getting a Job Game when you are the employer

Apart from knowing what skills and levels of experience are required for the role and prioritising their value, ask yourself also: what type of person do I need?

And then use language in your adverts, job description and person specification that will appeal directly to the personality you are seeking to attract.

For example, if you need a person who is motivated by following clearly established rules, write about the importance of procedures; present clear sequences, refer to well-proven methods and reliability. If you need someone who is drawn first to seeing and understanding the big picture, present a clear overview of the role and its place within the department or organisation; use simple sentences to write about principles and concepts. And if you are seeking to attract someone who prioritises products, systems, tasks or idea creation over relationship-building and/or people management, use impersonal pronouns to write about processes, goals and results.

Having studied all applications, short-list those who have the most relevant skills and experiences, and who use the phrases and language patterns that reflect the type of personality required.

Have the day planned thoroughly. Create a range of informal scenarios that will enable an appropriate range of staff to observe, meet and assess the applicants.

Remember, you are not only seeking to recruit a new colleague, you are also promoting your brand. Most of the applicants, and sometimes all of them, will end the day without having been offered the job; do everything you can to ensure they leave feeling and saying what you want them to about your business.

The Getting a Job game, as with all other conversations,

doesn't exist in a vacuum; plan for applicants' experiences with you to ripple out positively. So, when it's time to interview each candidate, do:

Manage the Introduction

If you are leading an interview panel, ensure that everyone understands all aspects of the interview procedure and behaves in the agreed manner.

Welcome the interviewee in a way that establishes the agreed tone, and then introduce all involved. Make clear the purpose and style of the interview, and how you will treat all information shared with you. Then:

Manage questions

As the interviewer:

- Determine the focus of your enquiry and rationalise the sequencing and framing of your questions.
- Ensure your questions are understood as intended by identifying the interviewee's preferred communication patterns and using those to frame your questions. (Unless you want to make life difficult for the interviewee so that you can see how they cope.)
- Keep questions short and simple.
- Give the interviewee time to warm-up and avoid asking key questions too early.
- Reframe questions if the interviewee doesn't understand them as required.
- As a general guideline, establish a listening/talking ratio of 80/20.

Manage closure

When interviewing, create a form of pre-ending as you would

in a presentation.[43] Let the interviewee know you have almost finished. An abrupt ending can leave interviewees wondering if they have made a mistake and you have stopped because of that.

Evaluate everyone's performance

This includes your own and all panel members, as well as the interviewees.

Whilst interviewers evaluate candidates against an agreed specification, there is often debate. If you are leading the panel, you might have the necessary power to force through your own decision. You might prefer, though, to exercise your communication skills rather than power in the ensuing debate. Many of the previous tips can be brought to play in this situation.

Provide feedback

Ensure the interview was a learning experience for all concerned. Provide interviewees with prompt, constructive feedback. In selection interviews, highlight what each interviewee did well and suggest ways to improve. Include the successful candidate in this process.

Time now to move away from recruitment and selection and on to:

Managing Meetings

Have you ever attended a meeting that didn't accomplish very much? Have you ever heard people rearrange the three words, 'time of waste.' when describing the value of a meeting?

It's interesting how damning those three words are whether they are said in that order or in reverse. A friend of mine, a

---

[43] More about that in Chapter Six.

nutritionist, tried to start a slimming club called, 'Time of Waist'. She was stunningly unsuccessful in attracting clients. I wondered if it was because of the negative way the words sound rather than look.

I had a meeting with my friend and explained that some words can be spelt the same and/or have the same pronunciation, whilst having different meanings. Such words are called homonyms. We talked about how these can be used in conversation to help us influence. She was incredulous.

'No weigh!' She said, acknowledging the plight of her business. 'Know way,' I replied, hoping she would.

When you are organising and leading a meeting

The following tips will help make your meetings time well spent. For obvious reasons, I won't repeat previous principles and tips like:

- Create the state before you operate.
- Communicate to others in the ways they like to be communicated to.
- Create positive more-the-more patterns.
- Sequence information appropriately.

Here are some new ones instead:

Ask yourself: Do we need to have this meeting?

There are two elements to this:

- Only hold meetings for which you have clearly defined positive outcomes.
- Ensure the timing of the meeting is ideal, or as close as you can get.

If you have any doubt about whether to call the meeting, evaluate the situation fully. If the doubt remains, save everyone's time.

Know whom to invite

There can be strategic, political and operational reasons for inviting people to a meeting. Know who needs to be there and why. Share the purpose of the meeting and your desired outcomes with them in ways that will motivate them to attend. Make sure they understand why it is important that they are present.

Prioritise agenda items

Put the most important items first, and limit the number. This guarantees that important issues are addressed when everyone's energy is high. It also increases the likelihood that, if you run out of time, the most important decisions will have been made. Inform those attending that the list is prioritised. This will help focus their attention.

Send the agenda and any accompanying documents at least several days in advance

You can use the agenda to make clear the purpose and desired outcomes of the meeting, as well as to identify the topics to be addressed. Give enough information and time to enable people to prepare thoroughly.

Determine the ideal duration

Be clear how long the meeting will last. Allocate just enough time. This creates a sense of urgency and focus.

Start on time, even if only one person is present. Otherwise, you risk letting others establish a more-the-more pattern you don't want. Also, do everything you can to limit the time spent reviewing minutes at the start of meetings.

Ensure you finish at the stated time, even if there are agenda items outstanding. If people are still engaged and energy levels high, they'll end the meeting wishing it had continued, and keen to return to the next one. If energy levels are dropping, the level of productivity will have already begun to diminish.

Whenever possible, end the meeting on a 'high'

People remember endings. So, although you can begin the meeting with a 'Hi', do aim to close your meeting on a positive note, with a good atmosphere and those involved feeling valued.

Of course, the atmosphere and state you need to create will be determined to some extent by the nature of the meeting. Aim for congruency. A meeting to discover the reasons for a recent drop in sales might require different attitudes and input than, say, a creative session intended to develop a new product.

Have clearly established rules of behaviour for all meetings. You might vary these according to the nature of the meeting. Whatever purposes your meeting serves, find a way to end well.

Send the minutes the day after the meeting

This gives people the opportunity to review them whilst the meeting is still clear in their mind. It also demonstrates your efficiency and indicates the importance you placed on the meeting.

Structure and present your minutes in a way that:

- Engage the readers' attention.
- Highlight the key points.
- Reflect accurately the points made and/or the decisions reached in the meeting.

Ask people to respond within a specified timeframe.

When you are invited to attend a meeting:

Prior to the meeting you might:

- Determine your own desired outcomes.
- Research fully; access all relevant information.

- Find out who the other attendees will be.
- Consider their likely responses to agenda items.
- Identify their relative levels of power and influence.
- Promote the value of your desired outcomes to influential others.

In the meeting itself you can apply many of the principles and tips we have already covered. You might focus particularly on:

- Matching, pacing and leading.
- Knowing when to focus on the big picture, when to talk about specific details, and when to remain silent.
- Creating appropriate more-the-more patterns.

Conflict resolution

Conflicts can occur for any of the following reasons:

Ideological differences

People holding incompatible beliefs, values and deep-rooted assumptions can come into conflict about the cause and/or the meaning of a situation, or the most appropriate ways to behave, or the most desirable outcomes. Or all of these!

If mismanaged, ideological differences can leave all parties involved feeling seriously misunderstood, under-valued, isolated or, even, vulnerable and threatened. These feelings can lead to increased tension and, at their worst, result in the most extreme levels of physical conflict.

Information mismanagement/misunderstanding

Conflicts can occur when people have access to different or insufficient information, or when they disagree about what shared information means. As I continue to highlight, communication is emotional first, so feelings about 'why you haven't shared this information with me', or 'why you don't understand what this data means', can negatively affect levels of trust and, even, turn collaboration into conflict.

Different interests

Parties with different interests and/or agendas can come into conflict over the best way(s) to resolve a situation and move forwards. Often, as each party prioritises satisfying its own needs, tensions can occur about access to, and the application of, essential resources.

Relationship mismanagement

Miscommunication is often the cause of conflicts in relationships, resulting in negative emotional responses, changes in perception, and a lack of trust.

Structural clashes

There are times when organisational structures encourage conflicts over available resources and opportunities for development. As with the other types of conflict, if the ensuing communication is mismanaged, the Me – You – Us approach will be lost beneath an ever-hardening Us and Them attitude. Engaging an unbiased mediator is one, important way of addressing conflict. Do bear in mind, though, that, even with such involvement, the skilful and respectful use of the power of conversations is at the heart of conflict resolution. Many of the attitudes, principles, skills and tactics previously identified, come to the fore when seeking to resolve conflict.

Let's take the first of our five examples, conflict caused by ideological differences, and consider how we might communicate to create resolution.

When a conflict occurs because a person, or group, feel that their beliefs, values and worldview are under threat or, at least, not understood nor appreciated, tensions can rise very quickly. Beliefs are powerful perception filters. Some of our beliefs are so deeply rooted, they form taken-for-granted, unthinking assumptions that determine how we perceive the world and how we expect people to operate within it. These most closely held beliefs are usually regarded as non-negotiable. Not least because of the fear that our worldview will collapse if we let them go. And without that, where would we be? And how would we know what to do?

It's no surprise, then, that conflicts caused by ideological differences can be so difficult to resolve to the satisfaction of all involved.

So, what are the attitudes, principles, skills and tactics we can use to chart our way through such a difficult situation?

They begin, as all skilled communication does, with a clear vision of what success will look like, and an understanding of the other's starting point (and their most likely desired end outcome).

The appropriateness of our desired outcome needs to have been confirmed by a rigorous ecology check; the fact that communication never occurs in a vacuum, is highlighted in this context, arguably more than in any other.

The ability to manage our own unhelpful perception filters about both the situation and those with whom we are communicating, is at once essential and, often, challenging.

An attitude of respect and sincerity needs to be expressed in ways that are most likely to be recognised as intended. And, whilst significant differences clearly exist between the parties involved, there are usually acknowledgements and affirmations that can be made at the beginning of, and throughout, the interaction. These might reflect the other's status, or sincerity, for example.

As ever, knowing what to match, how to pace, and when to lead is essential. As is a thorough analysis and understanding of the other party's beliefs, values, social norms, key influencers, personal, political and social agendas, their hierarchy of criteria, attitudes towards time, individual and social communication patterns, their perceptions of us and associated expectations. We can then incorporate:

- The application of the '*Yes and…*' mind frame.
- A willingness to transition from Me to You to Us.
- Recognising and responding to feedback.
- More-the-more patterns of agreement.
- Ways of creating and building commitment(s).
- The use of reciprocity.

Specificity is essential in this type of communication. So:

- Make clear what you can specifically acknowledge and affirm.
- Make clear what you specifically do understand, don't understand, or cannot accept – and why.
- Know where and how you can adapt your opening proposal if necessary.

Finally, use well packaged honesty throughout.

'Chris wastes time doing what he thinks he ought to. I just jump for joy.'

Delegation

For managers, the issue is not whether to delegate, but what to delegate and to whom. The starting point is to ask yourself, 'Is it essential that I do this task?' When the answer is 'No', consider delegating.

The recommendations in this section enable you to answer the following 'W' questions:

- What is the task I need to delegate?
- Why am I delegating it now?
- What quality of result do I require?
- When do I need the result by?
- Who will be delegated to the task?
- Why have I chosen this person?
- What is the nature of our relationship?
- What is the most appropriate form of control?

Define the task clearly

There are two elements to this. Firstly, understand the precise nature and purpose of the task, and the quality of the result that is needed. This also involves identifying the timeframe within which the task must be completed.

Secondly, communicate this clearly, using the communication preferences of the person to whom you are delegating the work.

Match the person to the task

Match the person to the task by answering these questions:

Can I use this task primarily as a learning exercise for someone?

If the result needs to be of the highest standard, the answer to this is probably 'No'. In which case, identify the most capable person to approach.

How can I ensure the person sees value in receiving this task?

Ideally, the person will benefit from the experience and will recognise those benefits. This means understanding their professional and, perhaps, personal goals, and having the ability to show how the task meets their needs as well as yours. Effective delegation creates a win-win situation.

What is the nature of our relationship?

Understand how the other person views you and your relationship with them. Their views will influence how they respond to your definition of the task, and your reasons for delegating.

Examine your own image and reputation and consider how it might impact on the other person. Will your presence be viewed as comforting or threatening? Determine if you are seen as a good mentor, or a good performer, or both.[44]

What degree of discretion will I allow?

Your answers to the previous questions will help you determine what form of control to employ. Factors that are of particular importance here are:

- The quality of the result that is required.
- The ability of the person.
- The personality of the person.
- The nature of your relationship.

The degree of discretion you allow when delegating work, and the form of control you employ, can influence the other person's level of motivation.

Some individuals might need and welcome constant support and supervision. Others might regard it as intrusive and insulting. Based on that, determine if you will measure progress throughout the work or if you will wait until

---

[44] To answer these questions accurately, you will need to be good at identifying and interpreting feedback.

completion, if you will you have regular meetings or if you will meet only if a problem occurs.

Aim for an approach that best reflects the nature of the task, the personality and skills of the person to whom you have delegated, and your relationship with them.

The final question to ask and answer is:

What deadline will I set?

Delegated work should be seen as a stimulating and relevant challenge. Setting appropriate timeframes has an important part to play in this regard. External factors might influence the deadline, as will the quality of the result required, the ability of the person, and your reasons for delegating to them. As the manager, ensure you prioritise the workload of the person you delegate to. Inevitably, when we delegate, we increase someone's 'to do' list and, if we fail to make clear what his or her priorities are, we risk creating unnecessary stress through work overload.

Develop your staff through delegation

Delegation can be viewed as an essential part of the manager's role because it provides opportunities for staff development whilst enabling managers to focus on their essential tasks.

Avoid upward delegation

This occurs when a colleague attempts to return responsibility for completing a task back to the manager who delegated it. Upward delegation limits opportunities for staff development and distracts managers from their essential tasks. Avoid upward delegation by defining the task clearly and matching the right person to the task.

As with so many things, the appropriateness and value of delegation is determined by our understanding of others and how we communicate.

Sam taught me about the value of delegation early on in our

relationship. Even as a pup, his instinct was to protect our house. Whenever anyone approached, he would yap furiously and then look at me for confirmation that he was doing the right thing. When I praised him, he would wag his tail and yap with even more vigour. I realised that, if he was to develop his guarding abilities to their full, I needed to make clear that the task was his, provide specific training and establish the boundaries within which he could operate. Sam welcomed both the training and the responsibility.

Now, when someone visits us, he barks loudly to make me aware, and then waits quietly to follow my lead. Every night, he wakes twice, and pads softly around the house making sure we are safe. He revels in this role and in the trust we place in him. When delegation works this well, everyone benefits.

'The only downside to this job is that I have to listen to Chris snoring.'

Telephone conversations

To be great at non-visual communication, you need first and foremost to be brilliant at listening. The essential things to listen for during telephone conversations are:

- The sound of the other person's voice and their

language patterns.
- Emotional indicators.
- Breathing patterns.

These aspects of communication are interconnected.

Unless we are highly trained, our emotional state usually influences our breathing, which in turn affects the sound of our voice, our choice of words and our language patterns.

The key sounds to listen for are the pace, tone, and volume of the other person's voice. Our aim is to match these subtly, being ready to adapt if they change during the conversation.

Emotional indicators are the most powerful form of feedback. Recognising the other person's emotional state and/or emotional changes creates the opportunity to respond accordingly. The aim is to match the other's emotion with the appropriate degree of obviousness or subtlety and to then either reinforce the emotion (if it is a positive one) or lead them away from it (if it is a negative one).

If the person we are talking to becomes very happy or excited, it's a relatively simple matter to join them in that emotion and, if possible, find ways to increase it. If the person shares an emotional response we don't want, the ability to exercise our emotional control and to then match with subtlety is paramount.

If, for example, the other person becomes unexpectedly angry we are likely to be emotionally affected. We might, perhaps, feel shock or surprise or concern, or feelings of failure. If we do, our first task is to dampen these down and return to our best communicating state. Only then can we respond well to the feedback we are receiving.

And if the person is sharing anger, we would usually avoid reflecting that same level of anger back. Instead, acknowledge it, match some of their communication patterns at a much lower level and, when it is appropriate to do so, begin the process of leading them into a more productive state.

With practice you can also learn to hear and match the other person's breathing pattern. This is both powerful and useful, no matter what emotional state the other person is experiencing.

Throughout the conversation adopt a *Yes and* approach, especially if your aim is to create dialogue, and listen out for words such as *but* and *try* that warn of disagreement or uncertainty. If your purpose is to gain acceptance for an idea, proposal, product or service, do apply any relevant principles of influence and create more-the-more patterns of agreement before asking for the other person's decision.

If, along the way, the other person falls silent because of something you've said you might:

- Remain silent yourself, at least initially.
- Give them time to construct their response.
- Offer a brief supporting comment, for example, 'Please, take as long as you need.'

Telephone conversations emphasise listening and speaking, whilst video calls add visual stimuli into the mix. Both require us to be fully present if we are to communicate, connect and influence as intended.

Conversations via video call

If you have time to prepare before leading or taking part in a video call, use the following three-fold approach:

Know your purpose

Determine your desired outcome. Then do your research about the other person or people, determine the language patterns, examples and sequencing that most suit their needs.

Rehearse

This is important because many of us feel at least a little awkward when talking on screen – especially when seeing ourselves on the screen as we do so! Given that, rehearsal must become a practical activity, creating the conditions that gradually increase adrenalin release and reflect the realities of a video call.

Manage your image

There are two essential elements of this. Firstly, dress to match the nature and requirements of the video call and ensure the environment that will be seen reflects your role and purpose. Secondly, determine how much of you will be on show and ensure the lighting is appropriate.

Managing your own image can help create the best personal state from which to operate, whilst also creating a positive first impression. Both are as important in this context as they are in every other form of communication.

With your preparation done, it's time to:

Manage the video call

In the moments before the video call starts, remind yourself of three things. Firstly, the need for alertness; be ready to communicate brilliantly from the first second you are seen. Think of how television presenters and newsreaders always begin talking confidently and clearly from the instant they appear on our screen. We never see or hear them warm up, they never stutter or stumble over their first words. Follow their lead.

Secondly, remember that you are either entering someone else's room, or you are inviting other people into yours. Treat the experience, therefore, as if you are actually in the room with everyone else. If you are a team leader, managing a video call with your staff, make sure they all treat it in this way, too.

Thirdly remind yourself to manage your facial expressions as well as your voice. Nod to show interest, agreement or engagement when someone else is talking. Express emotion with your eyes.

The world pioneer into the study of facial expressions is Dr Paul Ekman. His extensive research has revealed that some facial expressions and their associated meanings are universal. He discovered that, even people in societies that had never interacted with the outside world, such as tribes in the Amazon basin, used the same facial expressions as the rest of us to express certain emotions.

Ekman's work focuses too on what have become known as micro-expressions. These are essentially uncontrollable indications of emotion that flash across the face in a fraction of a second. Because we emote before we rationalise, micro-expressions provide a clear, although fleeting, insight into what we are truly feeling. They reveal the emotion we might decide to disguise, or the truth we might aim to deny.

Through training we can learn to recognise micro-expressions. Once developed, this greatly enhances our understanding of others and our ability to predict their likely responses.

In summary, then, managing our own facial expressions and interpreting accurately the facial expressions of others is an important part of influencing elegantly during video calls.[45] It's also integral to:

Delivering excellent customer service

Perhaps more than any other attribute, businesses lay claim to the high quality of their customer service. Perhaps, more than any other attribute, many businesses fail to deliver consistently to the standard they promise. And, perhaps more than any other attribute, great customer service is what we value most from those businesses with whom we engage.

Five elements combine to create great customer service. These

---

[45] And all other face-to-face interactions.

are:

- The consistent quality of the product.
- The nature of the business environment, virtual or otherwise.
- The effectiveness and efficiency of the organisation's systems.
- The quality and consistency of the communication between the staff.
- The quality and consistency of the communication between the staff and the customers.

Of these, the only element that can compensate for, and potentially even override, inadequacies with any of the others, is communication.

The simplest and most profound definition of service that I have ever heard was shared with me by Diego Masciaga, during one of our earliest interviews. He said, quite simply:

'Service is pleasing.'

All five elements mentioned above need to be in place if your goal is to please customers in ways that will bring them back to your business time after time and make them advocates of what you offer. Also, all members of staff need to understand that, either directly or indirectly, their primary concern is customer service. And all staff who communicate directly with customers need to be great at it.

As ever, this begins with having a clearly defined end outcome which, I would suggest, is to exceed the customer's expectations in ways that lead to repeat business.

In this regard, skilled attention-giving is necessary for accurate and swift pattern recognition. Identifying the customer's purpose and communication preferences are vital if rapport and feelings of ease and trust are to be created.

I mentioned in Chapter Three, how an unskilled salesperson

interrupted my buying strategy when I was looking at a suit; it's unlikely that I was the only potential customer to leave that day empty-handed because of inappropriate communication. And I'm not being critical here of the salesperson. I am, though, suggesting that the person who trained them failed to do a good job.

Whilst there are essential, underlying attitudes, principles, strategies and skills, the application of these is always bespoke. Whether engaged in customer service or not, we adapt our communication to match the preferences of the other; that's how we show understanding and respect. And how we increase our chances of achieving our desired outcome.

The principle that people buy from people, is at its most literal in the context of customer service. Feelings of being welcomed, listened to and understood, combine to put customers at ease. The more our communication can make things easy for others, the more likely they are to value our service and to engage with us further. If our communication fails, the 'good buy' that customers want to experience, often turns into the 'goodbye' that businesses don't want.

In The Introduction, we considered the potential costs to a supermarket of poor customer service due to miscommunication. That wasn't an exaggeration offered to make a point. Research estimates that businesses in the UK lose £12 billion every year because of poor customer service, and that inadequate service can cost brands as much as one-fifth of their annual revenue.[46]

Yet when the service and communication are good, research reveals that 71% of customers will then recommend the business to others and 44% will use it more frequently.

---

[46] It's estimated that businesses in the USA lose over $40 billion.

The communication that is central to providing excellent service begins before face-to-face interactions occur. It begins with the organisation's image, marketing and messaging, and can also involve any combination of online, email and telephone conversations. These communications create expectations that must be created and managed deliberately and skilfully. If they fail to create a sufficiently high level of expectation, customers won't visit in the first place. Yet, if customers arrive with expectations that cannot be met, they will leave disappointed.

Communication, then, is central in the process of expectation management, and this, in turn, is essential in creating what is regarded as great customer service. And it is great service that turns customer satisfaction into buyer delight.

How do you create that transition? The answer is in the following formula:

$$bd = cs + 1$$

In which:

bd = buyer delight.

cs = customer service.

$+1$ = The one way customers' expectations are exceeded.

When customers have their expectations met, they are satisfied; when their expectations are exceeded, they are delighted. The goal, therefore, is to ensure that at least some aspect of the product, environment, systems and, of course, communication, exceeds the customer's expectation in at least one way. At this point, satisfaction turns into delight.

Another truth when engaging with customers, is that occasional mistakes will inevitably occur. For the skilled communicator, these are unintended opportunities to surpass expectations. Once again, the *Yes and* approach is vital.

It encourages the following chain of events:

- The mistake is acknowledged.
- Ownership of it is accepted.
- The mistake is corrected.
- An extra benefit is provided by way of apology.

When this is done well, the resolution, rather than the original error, becomes the all-important take-away.

Which leads us to another important communication principle that has been mentioned already, and will be talked about again in the coming pages:

Endings really, really matter.

To ensure buyer delight, the interaction needs to end well. Too often, communication with customers ends poorly – even when the sale has been made.

Diego Masciaga's definition of service is profound because it reminds us to keep communicating with customers in ways that enhance their pleasure until they have left, not only until they have spent their money. A really good buy, ends with a really good goodbye. And, just like the greeting, it's at its best when it is heartfelt and skilfully honest.

We can only show genuine respect whilst serving customers, when the application of well packaged honesty runs through the entire interaction. In this context, it might be based upon the following principles:

- Pleasing comes before selling; the latter will grow out of the former.
- Only sell to the customer what is good for them and what they can afford to buy.
- Make the customer feel good about themselves and their purchase, irrespective of its monetary value.

Other communication processes, strategies and skills that help ensure great customer service include:

- Match – Pace – Lead.
- The Emotional Influence Flow.
- The OODA Loop.
- Communicating from the customer's learning side.
- Matching key words and phrases.
- Matching expressed needs and values.
- Creating more-the-more patterns of agreement.
- Avoiding the words, 'but', 'try' and 'don't'.
- Using the words, 'yes', 'and', because', 'just'.
- Knowing when to be silent.

Just as these strategies and skills extend well beyond the business world, so, too, does the value of service.

We can please others, by helping, supporting or providing for them in many different ways and in many different contexts. Family elders and parents can provide a most powerful service to younger family members and/or their offspring. Teachers and healers serve individuals and their communities. Members of the emergency services do the same. Military personnel are proud to serve. Whilst so many others in our societies, from engineers to bus drivers, from refuse collectors to park managers, serve in ways that might often go unrecognised, or be taken for granted.

Indeed, I would suggest that the quality of a society can, to a great degree, be measured by the quality of the service it encourages and maintains. And the quality of that service is influenced significantly by the quality of the communication involved.

That's true regardless of our position or role. And it's especially true if we are the leader.

Leading others

Much has been written about leadership; about the attitude, attributes, role, responsibilities and communication of leaders.

Here I'm only going to consider one specific responsibility. It's the ways in which the leader's communication, and the communication patterns and behaviours they allow from others, influence the wellbeing of individuals.

Communication affects brains in ways that create changes in emotional states, which, in turn, affect cognitive and physical performance.

As we have already considered, communication delivered by those regarded as authority figures, can be particularly influential. It follows, therefore, that leaders need to be highly skilled communicators who recognise that the quality of their communication influences far more than strategic direction, team cohesion and technical ability. It influences wellbeing.

Increasingly, organisations are addressing the topic of wellbeing by, for example, providing facilities for physical activity, offering classes in yoga and meditation, encouraging outdoor breaks and, even, providing private counselling sessions to help with personal, social or financial issues.

However, consistently inappropriate communication can undo any of the positive effects of such wellbeing practices.

Emotional management is at the heart of our ability to feel and perform well. Repeated communication that fails to demonstrate understanding or respect, that lacks clarity or any obvious desire for engagement, that creates confusion or stress, that demotivates, diminishes or devalues, that encourages division, that continually misuses the power of words, can impact negatively on performance and damage the wellbeing of people.

So, not only do leaders need to lead by example, ensuring that their communications influence positively, they need to make sure that everyone else is appropriately skilled.

And that everyone is mindful of how:

- Their interpersonal communication impacts the wellbeing of those around them.

- Their intrapersonal communication impacts their own wellbeing.

Beyond the need to Match, Pace and Lead, apply the OODA Loop, and create a desired influence flow, other principles, strategies and skills that are of value in this regard include:

- Knowing that influence is inevitable.
- Going first!
- Demonstrating the congruency that creates positive authority.
- Setting positive outcomes.
- Knowing how and when to ask the most useful questions, in the best possible way.
- Using inclusive language.
- Recognising and knowing how to appeal to the motivational tendencies of others.
- Recognising and knowing how to appeal to the decision-making tendencies of others.
- Telling stories that motivate, inspire and speak to peoples' experience.
- Creating and managing positive conversations.
- Knowing when to focus on the big picture; knowing when to focus on detail.
- Using the power of words to avoid and/or manage conflict.
- Remembering that:
  o The meaning of communication is the response you get.
  o People do things for their reasons, not ours.
  o People respond to their experience, not reality.

Leaders serve best by ensuring that the environments, systems and routines they create, combine with the power of their communication to enhance the wellbeing and, by extension, the performance, of all.

Sometimes, though, communication, and some conversations, are not spoken. Sometimes they are written. And when they are, they have a special power.

Chapter Five

Influencing using the Written Word

How to manage the written word positively and powerfully.

We all have opportunities to write and read. We do so using a variety of different formats, for a variety of different reasons. This chapter includes tips to help you prepare, plan, write, edit and speed read. We'll begin by developing three previous tips regarding inspiring environments, audience analysis and creating resourceful states.

Create a writing environment

As we have discussed, environments influence our emotional states and, consequently, our performance. Environments can, for example, inspire us, scare us, or make us feel comfortable and safe.

When my wife and I decorated our home last year, we didn't ask Sam for his advice. Likewise, I don't tell him how to arrange the blanket or toys in his basket. We both create environments that serve their intended purpose and/or reflect our mood.

When creating a writing environment, have all the materials and information you need at hand before you start writing.

Create an environment that inspires you to think, focus, write and be creative. Identify the colours, sounds, smells, amount of space, even the objects, you associate with being in a resourceful writing state. If you cannot recall a positive writing memory, remember a time and environment in which you were studying at your best. If that isn't appropriate, imagine an environment that will inspire you. Be specific and detailed. You are ready to write when you:

- Are in an inspiring environment.

- Have clearly defined positive outcomes.
- Have access to all relevant resources.
- Have created the necessary state within yourself.

Know what role(s) you are playing before you begin writing

For example, are you writing as the boss, or as an expert, an organiser, an information-sharer, a helper, or a storyteller? Or any combination of these?

Knowing this will help you to identify yourself to your readers. It will also help you determine the most appropriate writing style, the key messages you need to share, and, even, the nature of the response you expect in return.

If you are writing to someone you know, use language that reflects their preferred communication patterns. You can also match shared experiences, concerns, values and goals.

Most importantly, use your knowledge to focus on the readers' starting position, including their needs and expectations.

Unless the nature of your written communication absolutely prohibits it, write in appropriate multi-sensory language incorporating any, or all, of the above.

Know your desired outcomes before you begin to write

Have clear, positive outcomes from the very beginning. Only then can you begin to plan your document. And remember:

The written word doesn't change once it is in front of your readers

The written word can be changed during the editing process, yet once your document is in front of your audience, the words are fixed. Written words lack the adaptability of spoken words. The written word is both seen and, in many people's minds, heard as they read it.

The Japanese phrase 'Bunbu Itchi' refers to the power of 'the pen and sword in accord'. Very few of us carry a sword. We all have pens and computers. We all write. Because the written word is unchanging it has only one chance to share your message. When you have only one chance, you need to ensure your words cut through the noise as intended.

Your readers see what you have written before they read it

The presentation, structure and style of your document reflect the nature and tone of your content and help create the state you require within your readers.

Factors that determine the way the written word looks on a computer screen and/or in a written document include:

- Use of headings and sub-headings.
- Use of numbered paragraphs.
- Language use.
- Inclusion, and nature of, diagrams, pictures and charts.
- Font type and size.
- The type of paper; its feel, weight, texture and colour.
- The size of the document.
- Type of cover and binding.

How we dress reflects our mood, purpose, and role, even the expectations of others. Be clear whether your written communication should be sent out in jeans and tee shirt, or a business suit.

Organise and sequence your writing in the ways most likely to help you achieve your desired outcome(s)

Regardless of how you dress your writing, always determine the most appropriate ways to organise and deliver your content. This will be determined to a large extent by the topic you are addressing, the needs of your audience and the nature of the role you are playing. Managing concept, structure and use is one way of organising and sequencing information. Here are some others:

Sharing the big picture

Is it necessary to share the entirety of a situation with your readers? If so, determine when and how you will present the big picture. Ask yourself, for example, if there are obvious categories of information you can present to help define and explain the big picture. Are there ways you can simplify complexity?

Presenting small units of information

Sometimes it can seem as if there is just too much information to share. The challenge then lies in presenting it in small inter-related chunks. In these situations, begin by considering to what extent the information can be:

- Classified/Categorized.
- Compared or contrasted.
- Defined.
- Clarified through the use of analogy.
- Discussed within a cause-and-effect relationship.

Sequencing your information

When the sequence of events is a crucial factor in helping the reader understand the situation, use it to help you structure your document. Always remember that:

The order in which you sequence information influences your audience's responses and conclusions. [47]

---

[47] This is equally true when communicating verbally.

Identifying the process

Identify the different stages within the process being addressed and explain each in turn. Depending on the process, you might choose to explain:

- How to do something.
- How something happened.
- How something operates.

Having determined how to organise and sequence your communication, it's time to address decision-making and motivational tendencies. We'll begin by considering how to appeal to your readers':

Decision-making tendencies

Here are some examples:

Sensory preference

Does your reader reach a decision when something feels right? Do they need to read supporting information or see proof of previous success? If they need to hear about something to be convinced, should you even be writing to them? If it is a combination of factors, in what order do they prefer them?

Timeframe

Is your reader most influenced by past examples, or the promise of future achievements? Perhaps they give most attention to what is happening right now? Also, do you know how long it takes them to make decisions of the nature you require?

Frequency

How many relevant examples does your reader need to see or experience before they are convinced? If you can determine this, provide the required number.

The 5 W's.

These are:

- What?
- When?
- Where?
- Why?
- Who?

Answering the most relevant of the following 'W' questions will also help you identify decision-making tendencies:

- What information will be most important to my reader?
- What are their sensory preferences?
- What timeframes will they apply?
- When is the best time to give them my document?
- When are they likely to make their decision?
- Where are they likely to look for confirmation or a second opinion?
- Where can I direct them?
- Why will they be interested?
- Why do they need to be involved?
- Who influences them?
- Who can I refer to in my document to strengthen my case?
- What are the benefits that will most appeal to them?

If you know your readers' decision-making tendencies, you can appeal to them specifically. If not, include a variety of approaches. Then turn your attention to their:

Motivational tendencies.

Examples include:

Proactive/Reactive

Is your reader more likely to take the initiative, or wait until circumstances force them to act? Indeed, can your reader act upon his or her own initiative, or do they need permission or approval from someone else? Answers to these questions also help you determine if you are writing to the correct person.

Towards/Away from

Is your reader motivated by the opportunity to move towards something they regard as pleasurable, or away from something they deem painful? Do they want to achieve something new, or escape from something they regard as unpleasant, limiting, or just inappropriate? Do they respond best to the carrot or the stick? Once you know, you can frame your information and persuasion accordingly.

External/Internal reference

Does your reader rely on their own internal frame of reference to motivate themselves, do they turn to external sources, or do they use both? When you identify their preference, use it to help you frame your argument.

Match/Mismatch

To what extent does your reader instinctively identify similarities (matching), or differences (mismatching)? Or do they identify a mixture of the two (known as 'sameness with exception')?
By way of an example, look at the following diagram and tell yourself what you see:

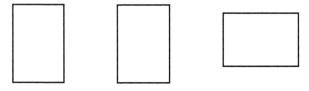

If you said something to the effect of, 'I see three rectangles', you naturally matched the images. You gave priority to the similarity.

If you said something like, 'One of the three rectangles is on its side,' you instinctively mismatched. You focused on the difference.

If you observed, 'There are three identical rectangles, with one on its side,' you recognised sameness with exception.

Our goal is to identify the reader's preference and then appeal to it specifically. When their preference is unknown, or when writing to several people with potentially different preferences, take a more varied approach.

General/Specific

Does your reader need to see the big picture first, or are they motivated more by the small details? This matters because if you present the information to your reader in their preferred order, your chances of influencing as intended increase.

Options/Procedures

When there are issues to be addressed, is your reader motivated to create options and seek out newness? Or do they instinctively turn to existing procedures? Knowing the answer will you help you decide whether to prioritise options or procedures in your document.

Priorities

Identify the readers' current priorities. Determine how you can best present your ideas, information or instructions in ways that reflect these.

Know when to be specific; know when to be artfully vague

There are times when you need every reader to receive the same message and supporting information. This requires you to be specific and detailed. There are other times when you need your written words to have different meanings for different people. This requires you to be artfully vague. Know when to switch from one style to the other.

Edit from third position

The resourceful state you create to draft your text, isn't the state you need to edit it. To edit you need a distanced, clinical approach. You let go of any emotional attachment you have to your work and operate instead with a sense of detachment. This state can be called 'third position'.

Whilst obviously not a writer, Sam is excellent at taking this position. For the first six years of his life, Sam had a four-legged companion and my cat, Louis, was not always a loving brother. Louis' initial caution when Sam first arrived changed to joyous domination once he realised that Sam had accepted him as the first amongst equals. Their relationship was based on the very firm foundation that Louis was the boss. At times he was a cruel dictator.

He loved to sit patiently, waiting for Sam to lay down near him. As he did, Louis dug his claws slowly and deliberately into Sam's cheek. Sam just remained still and looked for help. He had to be in pain. His instincts must have been screaming at him to treat the cat in the way dogs naturally do. He ignored them and chose third position instead. He distanced himself. Consequently, his feline brother lived a long, healthy life and died of old age rather than dog rage.

When writing, there are three perspectives we work from. These are:

- Our perspective as the writer.
- The audience's perspective.
- The editor's perspective - third position.

Firstly, as the writer, you determine your role, purpose, content, style and sequencing. Secondly, you identify your audience's needs, wants, experiences and expectations. Third position is removed from the other two and occurs after each draft of the work is complete. Using the editor's perspective, you ascertain how fully the text meets your purpose and edit accordingly.

Some writers edit in a different environment to which they write. It helps them assume third position more easily. So, too, does delaying the editing process. If you edit immediately after writing, you tend to see only what you expect to and so miss any errors. If possible, leave your work alone for at least several days before you edit. Then, when you do, use this simple step-by-step process:

- Read the entire document to ensure the sequencing and flow are as you intended.
- Check the spelling of individual words.
- Check the structure and meaning of individual sentences.
- Then do the same for individual paragraphs.
- Then do the same for individual sub-sections, sections and/or chapters.
- Read the entire document one final time.

You can also use third position to evaluate how well you have:

- Identified yourself, and your role, as the writer.
- Presented the document.
- Used the most appropriate structure, sequencing and style.
- Shown the big picture.
- Shared all relevant details.
- Used organisational patterns.
- Appealed to your readers' motivational tendencies.
- Appealed to their decision-making tendencies.
- Been appropriately specific and/or artfully vague.

Rewrite only when you have left third position and, once again, assumed your resourceful writing state.

Clearly, it makes sense to spend more time in third position editing an important business proposal, or a strategic report, than it does an informal email to a friend. Both, though, warrant some third position attention. The principle is simply this:

If something is worth writing down for others to read, it is worth viewing and editing from third position.

And finally, when you have a document to write:

Set and achieve deadlines

Begin by dividing your work into small tasks. Then give each small task a deadline. Be realistic in the time you allow. Understand all that is required of you. Allow for your other responsibilities. And, equally, respect the deadlines others are working towards. This is especially important if they are dependent on the document you are writing.

Focus throughout on producing a document that is only as good as it needs to be (or a little better if you want to exceed expectations). Write your drafts to the best of your ability, then edit to the required standard. Once that is achieved, resist any temptation to keep working. Whilst it requires discipline to write, it can require even more discipline to stop. Be disciplined.

Having said that, I'll stop talking about writing and turn my attention to a skill that will enhance your effectiveness and efficiency and save you that most precious of all resources, time. That skill is:

Speed reading

Before I teach you how to begin speed reading, let's just take a moment to consider how much time we spend reading – and, therefore, how much time we can save by being able to read more quickly and with greater recall.

Let's imagine a business manager called Stella. At work she spends on average four hours a week reading a range of material. That's sixteen hours a month, for the best part of eleven months every year.

If Stella learnt to double her reading speed (whilst simultaneously improving her recall), that would save her two hours a week. That's eight hours a month, the equivalent of a working day. That's over eighty hours a year, the equivalent of two working weeks. Over a career lasting thirty years that's 2,400 hours saved, the equivalent of sixty working weeks. In other words, during the course of her working life, Stella would have saved over a year of time.

As she is a married woman, with two children, an extended family and a full social life. I wonder how she might have spent that well-earned free time?

And doubling her reading speed is absolutely achievable! Which means that it's achievable for you, too. All it requires is a relatively small investment of time and effort.

The human eye is an amazingly effective creation. Human eyes recognise and decode masses of stimuli every second. Having said that, we do not read with our eyes. We read with our brain. The images that are decoded by our retina travel along the optic nerve before being sent to the occipital lobe, the visual area of the brain, which is situated at the back of the head. Why is this important? Because it emphasises the fact that biologically we are capable of reading far more quickly than most of us do. We are held back not by our physical capability, but by inefficient training and limiting beliefs.

We also know that our pupils change size according to the amount of light they are exposed to, the closeness of the object they are looking at, and the degree of motivation we feel.

Therefore:

- The more interested and excited you are about the

material you are reading, the more your pupils will dilate.

- The more your pupils dilate, the more words you will see at a single glance.
- The more words you see at a single glance, the faster you read.

If you want to excite your eyes, identify the benefits and advantages of reading the material, and create such an excited, motivated state that your entire body is affected.

The principle is:

Approach speed reading as you would any other vibrant opportunity.

You might feel the urge to pace the room, or to lick your lips, in anticipation. You might feel your heartbeat quicken. You might feel a smile spread across your face. Your mind and body are a system; let your physiological state reflect and, in turn, heighten your emotional state. Be excited!

If you understand the way your eyes work, you can begin, right now, to increase the speed with which you absorb written information.

When you read, your eyes make small jumps or hops from one point to another across the page. These movements are called 'fixations'.

Many of us see only a few words in each fixation. We then pause to recognise these words before moving on to repeat the process. For a non-speed reader, each pause can last for up to one and half seconds. The important point is that our eyes absorb the information during these pauses and not whilst they are moving.

Also, as our peripheral vision is highly developed, we can see many details that are to the right and left of our main focus of attention. This means we can develop the ability to see many words at once without moving our eyes from the centre of the page. And this provides the starting point for increasing our reading speed. We can do this substantially by:

- Increasing the number of words we see in each fixation.
- Decreasing the duration of each pause.
- Using peripheral and vertical vision.

The following techniques provide a simple and effective training method:

Technique 1

Use a thin guide, or a pointer, when you read. Move it in a smooth manner underneath the line you are reading. Begin by focusing on two-word fixations.

Technique 2

Shorten the length of each pause. When you reduce the time by just a fraction of a second, you increase your reading speed.

Technique 3

Increase the size of each fixation by adding an extra word to each movement your eyes make. When you can read comfortably and recall well focusing on two-word fixations, increase them to three words. When you are comfortable with that, look at four. Then five. With practice, you will be able to read one line in two fixations. When you can see an entire line in one fixation, simply put your pointer in the centre of the page and move it down.

Technique 4

Learn to read without sub-vocalising, which is saying the words in your mind as you read. Most of us tend to do this. Inevitably this slows down our reading speed because it means we can only ever go as fast as we can say the words. And we don't need to say and hear the words in our mind to understand them! Words are simply shapes that we give meanings to. We can recognise them in silence, just as we do most other things.

Take a moment now to look at whatever is around you. Be aware of the variety of stimuli, the different colours, shapes, movements, sounds and textures.

Are you having to tell yourself what each element is, what the different colours are, what the sounds and movements mean? Of course not. Actually, it would be a mind-blowing task. There is simply too much information to comprehend in that way. So, you simply look, recognise and interpret in silence. The best speed readers treat words in the same way.

Whilst techniques 1-3 will help you make great improvements in your reading speed, if you want to be really fast you have to stop sub-vocalising and look at words as you do every other shape.[48]

Technique 5

Avoid back-skipping. This is re-reading the phrase or sentence you have just read. Always ignore this temptation. Remember, and trust, the biological process by which visual stimuli are decoded and transmitted to the occipital lobe.

In tests, 80% of readers who were not allowed to back-skip discovered that the information had been understood and remembered, despite their fears to the contrary. So, once you start reading, keep going through the text until you reach your desired end point.

Technique 6

Practise skimming and scanning. When you skim a text, you look through it very quickly with the purpose of getting a general overview of the content and style. You scan to find

---

[48] How fast is fast? Set your sights on achieving speeds of at least 1000 words per minute, with excellent recall.

specific information. A useful way to approach an unfamiliar text is:

Prepare

Be clear about your reading objectives.

Preview

Spend approximately two minutes familiarising yourself with the content and style. Look at the contents page, chapter headings and sub-headings.

Active reading

Spend between 5-10 minutes skimming the first paragraph of each chapter you are going to read.

Read the text.

Use the techniques outlined to help you read as swiftly as possible. Speed reading not only saves time, it also improves our ability to recall what we have read.

Recall

Think about a time when you had to read and remember a text.

Did you slow down your reading speed in the mistaken belief that the more slowly you read the better you would remember? If so, did you find that you had to keep re-reading the text, because you were struggling to recall it? Did you find yourself getting bored and easily distracted?

If your answer is 'Yes', it's most probably because you were reading too slowly. When we are excited and motivated, we tend to speed things up. When we are getting tired and ready to sleep, we naturally begin to slow down.

If you want to test the effects of reading too slowly, simply choose a page of text and read it very, very, slowly. Say each word in your head s-l-o-w-l-y. See how far you get before you feel like, you know, yawning.

Now let's change the mood and consider:

The ideal reading environment

Whilst we can speed read anywhere, it makes sense to create the best possible environment when, and where, we can. Here are some key elements:

Light

The best reading light is natural daylight. If possible, therefore, place your desk near a window. If this is not possible, place a lamp behind you so that light comes over your shoulder opposite the hand with which you write. Have general lighting in the room also.

Chair and desk

Depending on your height, the desk should be approximately 20cm above the chair seat. The chair should encourage good posture by enabling you to have both feet flat on the floor and your back upright.

Distance from the text

Your eyes should be approximately 50cm from the page. This makes it easier to focus on groups of words and lessens the possibility of eyestrain.

And that's it for our introduction to speed reading.[49]   Once you have become a speed reader, I urge you to teach those you love how to speed read. You'll be giving them the gifts of enhanced effectiveness and efficiency, and more free time to spend as they choose.

---

[49] If you want to know more about speed reading and develop your ability even further, read: Buzan, T. The Speed Reading Book. 2009. BBC Active.

And so, in the blink of an eye, we come to the end of our time on the power of the written word. There's only one chapter left before we get into the pre-endings. This last one is about creating and delivering business presentations. I wonder how quickly you'll read it?

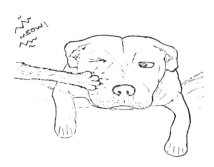

'Although that cat's stretching a point, even bare-faced cheek like this can be managed if you take the right position.'

Chapter Six

Influential Presentations

Conversations as performance art.

Epiah Khan wrote:

'Everything is a presentation if you care enough.'

I couldn't agree more. Presentations, like other forms of conversation, can be formal or informal in nature. They can be planned or spontaneous. They can have that communication-jazz style, or they can be more deliberately structured.

In this chapter, I am only going to focus on one type of presentation: those formal presentations we can be required to perform in the workplace.[50]

During the course of our career, and dependent on our role, we deliver business presentations for a variety of different reasons. These include:

- Selling. (A product or service, or our own abilities if it's part of the recruitment and selection process.)
- Leading change.
- Motivating staff.
- Educating and training.
- Promoting our business.
- Developing our network.

Presentations are an inevitable part of business life. The ability to present brilliantly influences business growth and career progression, it can help develop organisational culture and

---

[50] Again, much of the content in this chapter can be adapted and applied to other contexts.

create new clients. That's why we need to get them right. So, whilst many of our previous principles, process and techniques do apply, we are going to begin our consideration of presenting brilliantly with this:

Know your subject

Know it thoroughly and completely; know it from your perspective and from that of your audience. Know, too, that understanding your subject thoroughly is only the first step.

When it comes to presenting, the fact that you have content to share is a given. So, too, is the fact that you know this content. Your audience has the right to expect that of you.

Simply knowing your content is no guarantee that your presentation will be a success. That's why I said it's only the first step. What separates brilliantly influential presentations from those that are run-of-the-mill, is the way they are structured, sequenced and delivered. To do that brilliantly:

Know your audience and your environment

When Sam joined our family, a friend suggested that the first thing I should do was learn how to communicate in 'dog'. I found myself at a loss. I didn't know how to begin. The more I studied Sam, the less I felt I knew him. I asked my friend if he had any tips.

'If you want to understand Sam,' he said without hesitation, 'you need to communicate on his level. I mean that literally.'

So, I got down on my hands and knees and mimicked, observed, and played with my dog. It was a delightful education. I not only came to know Sam, I also saw the world from his perspective. It was invaluable.

When planning a presentation, you can learn how to communicate in your audience's language without having to get on your hands and knees. Aim to gather the necessary information regarding the audience make-up, expectations, knowledge of the topic, assumptions and, if possible, personal agendas. Know their needs, wants and likes and use this information to help you plan your presentation.

Also, visit the venue prior to your presentation. Or, at the very least, arrive early. Spend some time getting a feel for the place; make it your own. Check that it has the equipment, technical support, space and atmosphere you need. If possible, rehearse there.

Rehearse your presentation

Think of business presentations as performance art for the business professional. They are exercises in skilled, attentive messaging. If you want to deliver a great performance, it is wise to rehearse.

When you cannot rehearse in the actual venue, have a final rehearsal in a space very similar to the one you will be in. Ask critical friends to watch several of your rehearsals and offer feedback. Film yourself. Time yourself. Be in your resourceful state when you rehearse.

Rehearsing not only gives us the confidence that comes from knowing our content, it also helps us to develop:

Messenger congruency.

When delivering presentations, we need to be seen (and heard) as the right person for the topic. The more we develop the ability to deliver and perform a presentation well, the more likely it is that the audience will accept us as the best possible messenger. When this happens, our capacity to influence as intended increases significantly. And to maximise that capacity, we need to appreciate that:

Presentations begin before they begin

They begin when you are first invited to present. At that time, create the resourceful states you need to plan, develop and rehearse your presentation.

Planning begins with the writing of the:

This is the compelling story you simply have to tell. Like all good stories, it needs to be engaging, emotional and relevant; it needs to appeal to your audience.

Facts and figures alone don't influence people in the way that stories do. Especially stories that educate, entertain and inspire; stories that offer solutions, benefits and truths, stories that speak to, and of, the audience's experiences and needs. Facts and figures have their place within such stories: they act as proof points and help the storyteller gain the audience's trust. The story comes first though, so make sure it's great!

On the day of the presentation, assume your resourceful state before you arrive at the venue. If you spend time with audience members before your presentation starts, treat it as you would a conversation in a corridor: share messages and prime them for what is about to follow and how you want them to be.

Priming simply means using words, or any other stimuli, to influence someone's future behaviour – usually without them being consciously aware of it. If, for example, I remind you of the story about my doctor that I shared with you in Chapter Three and then ask you to unscramble this word:

nrsue

you will probably do so swiftly because the word 'doctor' primed you.[51]

Apart from what we say, we can also place images and objects in the environment to help us prime our audience, and we can use any written communication that we send ahead of time to do the same. Then, when the time comes:

---

[51] It primed you to think of 'nurse'.

Begin the presentation with at least one Pre-Introduction

The purpose is to:

- Get the audience's attention.
- Create the most appropriate atmosphere in the room.
- Establish your role and control.

Your pre-introduction(s) can be as simple or as creative as you choose. The simplest way is to introduce yourself (or have someone introduce you in a manner of your choosing), then welcome the audience and tell them how much you are looking forward to presenting. If you decide to include a more creative approach, do ensure it reflects the purpose and content of your presentation and, if possible, is something you can return to, and give greater significance to, as your delivery progresses.

No matter what type of pre-introduction(s) you employ, only begin the actual presentation when the audience is in the required state and are fully focused on you.

The Introduction follows the Pre-Introduction

In the introduction, outline what is to follow. Think of your presentation as a journey that is clearly sign-posted from the outset, rather than a mystery tour. People on a mystery tour divide their attention between exploring their current situation and wondering where their final destination might be. Your audience needs to know where it is and where it is going, so share the route before you branch out into the main body of your presentation.

The Main Body of your presentation follows the Introduction

Here you share the main part of your story, incorporating key information and justifying your most important points. Do:

- Use an appropriate mix of visual, auditory and

kinaesthetic language, when sharing your key points.
- Vary your sequencing of concept, structure and use.
- Provide supporting examples that are relevant to your audience.
- Satisfy the audience's needs before their wants; their wants before their likes.
- Highlight benefits.
- Create seamless transitions from one element of your presentation to the next.

You can also:

Use a mixture of techniques to help you create states and to support your message and style

Begin by deciding which combination of techniques will be most appropriate for each presentation. Here are a few suggestions:

Questions

If you ask your audience a question during your presentation, make it clear whether or not you want an answer. Either way, do still give them time to decide what their answer is.

Questions are useful because, even if answers are not spoken out loud, they inevitably engage minds. With practice you will see which senses people are using as they explore your question and determine their answer. You can then adapt your language, if necessary, to meet their preferences. And, if you do encourage the audience to share their answers, you gain actionable insight into such things as their knowledge, hopes, concerns and agendas.

Two-part contrasts

Phrases that combine a contrast are remembered easily. So, don't ask what your presentation team can do for you. Ask only what you can do for your presentation team.

Puzzle-solution formats

Offer your audience a puzzle and give them just enough time to consider the solution. Puzzles, like questions, engage minds.

Position-takers

Outline a situation about which the audience would expect you to have a view. Then tell them your position and justify your thoughts.

Silence

To be silent for a second or two after making a significant point, or asking a question, or telling a joke, implies confidence. Used appropriately and sparingly within a presentation, silence and stillness can speak volumes.

Humour

Use humour only if the situation allows it. Ensure the humorous content is relevant and acceptable to your audience. Ideally it will do more than just make your audience laugh. For example, when sequenced well, humour can be used to emphasise the importance of the serious point you make when the laughter stops. (In this regard, humour becomes a deliberate part of an emotional influence flow.)

Change states

Manage your own state first. Ensure you are in the required state throughout the presentation. This is the state from which you can present and perform at your best, whilst monitoring the audience's reactions and being able to respond accordingly.
You can change the audience's state in a variety of ways and for a variety of reasons. Here's an example:
I once ran a communications workshop and enjoyed dinner with the participants the night before. They were clearly looking forward to the next day.

When the workshop began, I made a host of communication errors in the first ten minutes. Their sense of excitement and anticipation changed into a mixture of irritation, embarrassment and, in some people, obvious concern for me as they realised that I wasn't up to the job.

When I stopped and asked them how I was doing, many of them changed into a state of uncertainty and confusion; unsure if, or how, they should best respond.

Then, when I told them I'd been making mistakes deliberately, their mood changed again, this time to one of relief.

Finally, when I told them I had made precisely seventeen communication errors, and their first task was to get into groups and identify them all, they changed again. Now curiosity took over as they sought to determine the seventeen.

Whenever you decide to deliberately manage the audience's state throughout your presentation, ask yourself the following questions:

- What emotional and physical state do I want my audience to be in when I share this particular piece of information, or this argument, with them?
- How can I create that state?
- How will I recognise it?

When delivering the presentation, monitor the audience's state continually. Ask yourself, 'Is this the state that I want them to be in right now?' If the answer is 'No', take immediate action to change it.

Mark space

Use different areas of the stage consistently to create different states within your audience. If, for example, you are going to be humorous three times during your presentation, do so from the same place. If you have four key points that you need your audience to consider seriously, make them from a common, but different, place. And so on.

This is another example of priming because, if you create these associations, your audience will unconsciously begin to change state as you move to a particular space.

The rule of three

If you need to make a series of points, or provide a series of examples, offer three. Why three? Because:

- If it is an important topic, you should be able to find three strong examples with relative ease.
- Three examples give your audience enough to think about without risking information overload.
- Three well-chosen examples should ensure that at least one of them is of relevance to each audience member.

You can also use the rule of three to embed commands. Simply ask your audience to do two things you know they are going to and follow these immediately with a third request to do something they might not otherwise have done. For example, whilst presenting you might say:
'I'd like you to look at the next slide…' (This is the first unnecessary command, as your audience would have done so automatically.)
'…And read the model it shows in a clockwise direction as indicated…' (If it is indicated, the audience would, again, have done so without prompting.)
'…Then consider the most significant benefits of our proposal to your organisation'. (Finally, the instruction to do something they might not have done.)
This is another example of a more-the-more pattern. If someone finds it easy and natural to do the first two things you ask, they are far more likely to do the third.

Imagery and Metaphor

Myths, metaphors, physical objects and descriptions of a possible future, can all be used to engage your audience, change their state, and help them remember your key points. Make your choices creative, engaging and relevant.

Visual aids

Only produce visual aids if you are certain that you need them. And always have a back-up. Technology does let us down occasionally, so have at least one additional set of visual aids.

If you do create visual aids make them clear, simple and easy to understand. Only show information that relates directly to what you are talking about.

As a general rule, do talk with your back to the screen. This sends out a message about how well prepared you are and how well you know your topic.

Also, make your presentation as multi-sensory as possible. The more senses people use, the more stimulated they are.

If you choose to use particular objects as visual aids, decide how, when and why you want your audience to first see them.

Finally, remember that you are the most important visual aid in the room. How you look, speak and move is at the centre of everyone's attention.

Provide at least one Pre-Ending

Pre-ending(s) follow on from the main body of your presentation and let your audience know that you are coming to the end. Unless you are presenting to someone on their birthday or at Christmas, it pays to avoid surprises.

At the beginning of this book, I asked you to consider the numerous pre-introductions airports and airlines use as they prepare us for our flight. They make good use of pre-endings also. Just consider how the Captain always lets us know that we are beginning our descent, and then how the cabin crew begin to change their, and our, behaviours, and how the Captain then provides updates about the weather at our destination, before we are eventually told to fasten our seatbelts. By which point tourists are already looking out of the windows and business travellers are sat back, mentally preparing for the meetings that lie ahead. Airlines know that highlighting and easing towards the ending is an essential part of the flight.

It's essential in presentations too because, as I've mentioned before:

Endings are really, really important

Think of your favourite novel or film.

Did it start well? I guess so, or you might have given up immediately. Did it keep you gripped as the story unfolded? I'm pretty sure it did, otherwise you would have lost interest. Did it have a great ending? I'm certain the answer is 'Yes'. If you thought the book or film was great and then didn't like the ending you would have been very disappointed.

Ensure your presentation has a great ending by summarising your key points, reminding the audience why your argument is so powerful, and then adding something extra. Something that fits perfectly. Something that touches your audience in an unforgettable way, that creates a positive emotional response and makes them thirst to take the action you need them to.

Finish on time

Brilliant time management is a mark of professionalism and respect. It emphasises how well rehearsed your presentation has been.

Make the audience ask at least some of the questions you want them to

You can do this in a variety of ways. For example, you can leave one aspect of your talk under-developed, making it clear that you would be delighted to discuss it further during the Q&A. Alternatively, you can raise a question during your presentation, and not answer it fully. Or you can use your knowledge of the audience to help you guess their most likely questions. You can then choose to answer only the majority of them during your presentation.

If you are presenting with a team, ensure that everyone is prepared to answer specific questions. If you are asked an unclear question, seek clarification.

Evaluation

As with recruitment interviews, spend time reviewing your performance. Take notice of your gut-feeling immediately afterwards and combine that with a more clinical approach a couple of days later.

And finally, do remember always that a presentation is not a natural interaction. It is a performance that requires planning. Aim to make your presentations emotionally and logically compelling. Engage your audience through the simplicity of your structure and the quality of your high-level performance skills.

Just be brilliant.

'Mark space? Who do you think he learned that from?'

Pre-ending No.1

A world of conversations.

'Ladies and gentlemen, this is your author speaking. We are just beginning our descent towards the end of this book. We expect to arrive in approximately six-and-a-half minutes.[52] Conditions are excellent and, after this pre-ending, all our content is Sam-focused. So, please sit back, relax, and, if you care to look out of your window, you will see a world filled with conversations. I hope you enjoy the rest of your journey.'

I made the point early in our time together that communication fills – and moves and changes – our world. The world of interpersonal communication, I said, is the world; it is happening all around us. We are an influential part of it. Our very presence makes a difference.

And the fact that all forms of communication, and every type of conversation, are going on endlessly, is great news if we desire to improve our value as a partner, parent, friend, neighbour, community member, leader, colleague, teammate, mentor, teacher, or any of the other roles we play in our complex lives.

If we want to sharpen our ability to listen, or develop our visual acuity, or improve how we talk or use the written word, our communication-filled world never stops offering us opportunities. We don't have to buy some special training clothes, or visit a special place, to practice. The world, quite literally, is our communication gym. We can workout anytime.

---

[52] That's because studies suggest the average reading speed for adults is between 230 and 260 words per minute depending on the content, and there are just over 1500 words left to read. (Unless, of course, you have already learnt to speed read; in which case you'll reach the ending more quickly.)

And when we do, if we get it right, our influence can be irresistibly good.

As the story in our second, and final, pre-ending highlights.

Pre-ending No.2

The story of Sam and the boy who cried before he laughed.

My nephew, Peter, was six years old when he came to visit and hurt his foot.

No one was quite sure how he did it. One minute he was chasing an imaginary foe in the back garden. The next minute, as best we could tell, his imaginary foe had tripped him up. Peter howled. We all rushed outside. Sam sat down when I told him to and waited for the humans to repair the situation.

Peter's mum rushed forwards, joined him on the floor, hugged him to her chest and began whispering soothing words. I couldn't hear what she was saying, but it clearly didn't help. Peter bawled even louder and drizzled snot down her blouse. The more she hugged, the more he screamed. Eventually, she released her hold, fell silent, and sat back. Her right hand rested gently on her son's shoulder as she considered what to say and do next.

Peter curled into a ball and clutched his ankle.

Peter's father stepped up. He opted for a more forensic approach. 'Let me feel your ankle, son.' He said, kneeling down and reaching out with both hands.

The hedgehog that was Peter curled tighter and squealed loudly when his father touched him. It brought the forensic examination to an abrupt halt.

Peter's mum glared at her husband. He straightened and raised his hands in submission.

My wife looked at me. 'Let's go make some tea,' she said.

We saw what happened next through the kitchen window.

Sam slowly inched his way towards Peter. Sam's ears were drooped, his tail was tucked between his legs. He shivered slightly. He lay down next to Peter and whimpered. For several minutes they lay there. The boy crying. The dog whimpering.

Only, as I watched, I realised that Sam was whimpering less, and Peter was crying less.

As Sam stopped shivering, Peter let go of his foot. When Sam's body relaxed, Peter straightened. Sam sat up. Peter followed suit. Sam's ears pricked and his head cocked to one side. Peter smiled. Sam licked his face. Peter giggled. Sam jumped to his feet, inviting a game of tag. Peter laughed out loud and began the chase, his pain and misery a thing of the past.

Peter's parents joined us in the kitchen. His father said, 'Your dog has done what none of us could. Just what do you call that?'

'Elegant,' I said. 'Simply elegant.'

'When we walk in the park, Chris notices more than ever. He used to think that nature repeats itself, so he didn't listen and look with curiosity and joy. Now, like me, he treats every walk as a new adventure!'

The Ending

Sam.

As we come to the end, I have two final things to share with you. They are both lessons from Sam.

The first takes us back to the topic of attitude.

I've saved what I regard as the most important part of a communicator's attitude for the end of our time together.

That part is:

Gratitude.

It was the first thing Sam ever demonstrated to me. From the start of our relationship, he showed me how to feel and demonstrate gratitude for even the smallest of experiences and opportunities. He showed me how forgetfulness deletes expectation and how the space that's left is best, and most easily, filled first with gratitude.

Sam has always been so busy living in the moment he's never had time for expectation; he's never allowed himself to be distracted by unnecessary comparisons. And this, I've come to realise, is one of his greatest lessons. Before Sam, I'd never been taught how to manage comparisons. He helped me appreciate the need to do so. The way I understand it now is that there are essentially three types of comparison. These are:

- Appropriate.
- Inappropriate.
- Irrelevant.

Appropriate comparisons are those we can learn from. They motivate and inspire. They enable us to grow and build as individuals, families and/or communities. They have an important role to play in the transition from Me to You to Us.

Inappropriate comparisons create the opposite effects. They diminish, divide, damage or destroy. They lead us to dangerous and flawed conclusions. They can make an individual decide they are not capable or worthy. They can make individuals and groups certain of their superiority. They prevent the connectivity and respect upon which elegant, ethical communication is based.

Irrelevant conclusions can also lead to division, and they inevitably create distractions that waste our time.

Sam avoids these comparison-traps. He's taught me how inappropriate and irrelevant comparisons inevitably limit our gratitude for the myriad opportunities to communicate, connect and learn that life offers us. And, every time we walk in the park, he models how genuine curiosity prevents the temptation to make such comparisons.

Sam is grateful for the slightest touch and the briefest word of acknowledgement. He's grateful for the trust we place in him whenever he plays with our grandchildren. He's grateful for every opportunity to walk by my side, and he approaches every interaction with his wonderful mix of curiosity, enthusiasm and joy.

Gratitude, I have come to realise, is the feeling that makes all those other feelings possible.

We can't be joyous if we're not truly grateful in the first place. Our curiosity and enthusiasm will be limited if we're not grateful for the opportunity to interact with someone and learn something new. And this is at the very heart of successful communication.

Also, when seeking to use the power of conversations, remember that listening is the primary skill. Then, when it's time for you to speak, remember that:

It isn't what you want to say, it's what the other needs to hear, that matters most.

And that:

So, get your breathing and the pitch, pace and tone of your voice right, and use this as the delivery system through which to match the language of others.

Going first means feeling grateful for the chance to use and share the power of conversations. From that starting point, the giving of skilled attention, the deliberate forgetting of our own perception filters, the desire to understand and influence eloquently and with integrity, all come to the fore more easily and readily. And then the magic of great communication can happen!

Which leads us on to the second thing I want to share with you. It, too, is a development of something from a previous chapter. I mentioned near the beginning of our time together that Sam and his brothers and sisters have had some bad press in the past. Consequently, when we're walking in the park, there are those who keep well away because think they know all about him.

A blinkered, casual glance does nothing more than reinforce an existing bias. A Communication Magician knows how to listen and look with far greater acuity than most; their interaction is driven by genuine curiosity and respect, seeking a level of insight that enables them to hear and see below the surface.

Sam, just like the rest of us, is worthy of such focus. In fact, if you look closely, you will realise that Sam has been at the heart of this book, sharing the most important messages with you, in ways that go far beyond my stories about him or his appearance in the cartoons.

Here, as we move towards the end, are the pages on which Sam appeared and the lessons, and reminders, he offered:

Page 9

Why our communication, whether transactional or

transformative, is always **s**hared **a**nd **m**eaningful.

Page 14

Our essential equation: **S**timulus + **a**ssociation = **m**eaning.

Page 34

How our communication DNA is based upon a **s**trong, **a**ligned **m**otivation.

Page 48

The importance of, and relationship between, **s**ilence **a**nd **m**editation.

Page 108

Why, and how, influence begins by **s**ensing, **a**cknowledging and **m**atching.

Page 185

The importance of **s**killed, **a**ttentive **m**essaging.

And finally:

Sam was with us from the very beginning. He was there even before the obvious Pre-Introductions. He was there, beneath his picture on the front cover. He was your first, and he is now your final, reminder of the **S**cience, **A**rt and **M**agic of transformational communication.
And with that said, I have to go.
It's time for another walk in the park.

Chris